The Old Church on Walnut Street
A Story of Immigrants and Evangelicals

# The Old Church
## on
# Walnut Street

# A Story of
# Immigrants and Evangelicals

by Chris Price

The Digital Press at the University of North Dakota
Grand Forks, ND

Book Design: William Caraher
Cover Design: William Caraher


Digital Press at The University of North Dakota, The
ISBN-13: 978-0692057575
ISBN-10: 0692057579


Library of Congress Control Number: 2018900946
Digital Press at The University of North Dakota, The, Grand Forks, ND

# TABLE OF CONTENTS

I first began work on the first edition of this short book a little more than six years ago. I had no idea what direction the study would take after getting approached to write about this old church that was about to be torn down. I decided to investigate the people who met in the building over the course several decades, because without people, the structure itself was a rather simple building that did not fall far outside of the ordinary for its day or its neighborhood. An ornate cathedral with magnificent stained glass windows or gothic arches carved from massive stones it was not.

Upon looking into the people who worshiped in the old Trinity Lutheran building, the place of the original congregants as immigrants readily became evident. The origins of the church in the latter nineteenth century was dominated by the Norwegians who came to North Dakota Territory, and later the State of North Dakota, in search of a better life. Historically speaking, this period saw what has come to be known as new immigration.

This era led to an upsurge in nativist sentiment throughout the United States. These bouts of anti-immigrant attitudes and activities have come about periodically throughout the history of the US. In the 1840s, the Irish were the source of much scorn from the broader society that was largely dominated by those who were white, Anglo-Saxon, and Protestant. In the latter nineteenth and early twentieth centuries, animosity from WASPs fell on the Chinese (leading to the Chinese Exclusion Act of 1882) as well as those who came from Southern and Eastern Europe. The Norwegians were not generally a major source of nativist objections, but others were. These "new immigrants" included people who were from Italy, Greece, Russia, and other regions of Europe where residents spoke Slavic languages.

These new arrivals generally had light pigmentation like the WASPs, but they did not speak English. Additionally, their religious loyalties tended to fall outside of the Protestantism that dominated much of America at the time. Many were suspect because they belonged to Christian traditions such as Roman Catholicism and various regional forms of Orthodox Christianity. Others, largely from Slavic lands, were not even nominally Christian at all, but rather Jewish. There was a great fear that Catholics could not be good Americans because their ultimate loyalty centered around what the Pope in Rome decreed instead of the ideas embodied in documents like the Declaration of Independence or the Constitution. This fear of Catholics continued during the Progressive Era and on through to the eventual election of John F. Kennedy in 1960.[1]

The US appears to have entered, or at least plunged deeper into, another round of nativism since the first edition of this book appeared in 2012. Donald Trump opened his run for the presidency in 2015 with a promise to build a border wall between the United States and Mexico. His reasoning noted, "The U.S. has become a dumping ground for everybody else's problems…When Mexico sends its people, they're not sending their best…They're sending people that have lots of problems, and they're bringing those problems with us. They're bringing drugs. They're bringing crime. They're rapists. And some, I assume, are good people."[2]

This view of certain immigrants as a danger is nothing new. James G. Blaine, a Senator from Maine who ran as the Republican presidential candidate in 1884, opposed the immigration of the Chinese in the Senate, arguing that "Either the Caucasian race will possess the Pacific slope, or the Mongolian race will possess it…The Asiatic cannot live with our population and make a homogenous element." He then argued that the Chinese had "no regard to family," nor did they in his estimation recognize marital or parental relations as the Europeans who came to North America did.[3]

The famed evangelist Billy Sunday held similar views, although he expressed them in a less formal manner than did Blaine:

I would knock into a cocked hat and higher than Gilroy's kite the theory, sir, that America has got to be forever the dumping ground for foreign filth. I mean the class that no other country wants. The devil himself would not have them. They have got the instincts of a dog without his fidelity. That is the bunch I mean. Say, we have made American citizenship too cheap: we have allowed every creature that calls himself a man and wears whiskers and poses on his hind legs to sway the scepter of American sovereignty and become a factor in framing public opinion. We have made 'er too cheap. I tell you. You are suffering for it right now...

> That is all we ask, yes, sir: but we can't compete with this promiscuous importation nowadays. An American has got to have meat once a day and a bath once a week. You can't compete with a fellow who takes up his belly-band for breakfast, no; eats spaghetti and hot dog and rye bread for lunch, and sucks in his limburger cheese for supper. No, no sir.[4]

The words uttered by Blaine and Sunday seem very familiar to some that are common in present-day public discourse. Many Americans seem to worry that recent immigrants are only coming for taxpayer-funded social services.

Another fear that the new immigrants of years past aroused was the belief that many held radical political beliefs that threatened society. Events like the infamous 1886 Haymarket Riot, after which five German-born immigrants were charged and found guilty, seemed to verify their fears. Even the small town in West Virginia where I spent my formative years saw Italian immigrants drawn to socialist ideas during the mine wars that occurred in the first couple of decades of the twentieth century.[5]

When looking at the immigrants from more than a century ago, however, one thing that is striking is the fact that most of their descendants assimilated strikingly well and fairly quickly into mainstream American society. The aforementioned John

F. Kennedy is a notable example who rose to hold the highest office in the land. Some of the family names of the Italians who were prominent in the West Virginia mine wars noted above are names that are familiar from my youth. A few of the descendants of these Italian immigrants even did such a good job of assimilating that they left their native Catholicism for the Baptist church that I attended for more than two decades.

The study of Trinity Lutheran shows this process of assimilation actually taking place over a number of years, as the Norwegian Lutherans in the Grand Forks community who initially worshiped as the Zion Lutheran congregation split largely over linguistic concerns and the adoption of American culture. This initial split took place in 1893, which was just fourteen years after the founding of the first Norwegian Lutheran church in Grand Forks. By 1918 Zion Lutheran and Trinity Lutheran agreed to hold services in both English and Norwegian, and in 1921 First Lutheran, which initially began as an ill-fated attempt to maintain Norwegian heritage, shifted to using English exclusively. By the time the three congregations merged into United Lutheran in 1926, the adoption of English by the Norwegian-Americans was complete. Today, those who might happen to drive by United Lutheran with no prior knowledge of its immigrant past or its affiliation with the Evangelical Lutheran Church in America will see little in its Art Deco façade that would indicate that Norwegian-Americans founded it. A similar experience might be had by those who happen to visit a church that is a part of the Converge movement. This network of churches was formerly known as the Swedish Baptist General Conference and more recently as the Baptist General Conference after English became the language of choice in this religious tradition that had early Swedish roots.[6]

With few exceptions such as Anabaptist groups like the Amish and the Hutterites (the latter of which one can still hear speaking German while on trips to Wal-Mart and other retail establishments in Grand Forks and other towns on the Northern Plains), this pattern of assimilation over two or three generations is common throughout American history. One has to wonder if the immigrants who are the cause of so much concern today will become the pillars of society in the decades to come. Will they take up positions of leadership, much as people like the Kennedys, or even President Trump himself, have? Will they adopt American culture in many ways, while simultaneously contributing to it in others? After all, who can imagine Manhattan without Little Italy or San Francisco without Chinatown? Will these immigrants become more secularized or take up more traditional American religious beliefs over time? Only time will tell, but if history is any guide, the prospect is quite likely.

Another theme that is common through much of history is related to the men and women who never reach the spotlight. The two churches that inhabited the building on Walnut Street were made up of individuals who are mostly unknown to the historical record. The names of the pastors and a few prominent laypeople who served these churches are known through the histories that the congregations felt compelled to write. A couple of the early members of the Grand Forks Church of God rose to positions of prominence that did much to impact their broader religious movement. Most of the rank-and-file parishioners are not known to us, however.

This does not mean that these unknown people were unimportant. Many of them no doubt attended meetings, contributed finances, and otherwise served their respective congregations in various ways. These congregations provided religious instruction, hope for the afterlife, and a sense of community for those who belonged to them. At times, they branched out in an attempt to contribute to the broader Grand Forks community as in the prominent cases of the Signing Christmas Tree and the live nativity scene that the Church of God provided before the 1997 flood contributed to that congregation's move from the Walnut Street property. My hope is that as readers engage with this short book, they will remember that these early, largely anonymous immigrants did much to contribute to the world we inhabit today, and communities like Grand Forks are much richer for their efforts.

Chris Price
Colby, KS

FORWARD
By Bret Weber

A community's memories and stories provide the building blocks for understanding its present and envisioning the future. This is not mere sentimentality or starry-eyed romance: an informed, objective understanding of a community's past is essential to its financial future, efforts to provide safety and well-being, and in creating the sense of belonging that engenders pride of place. A respectful understanding of the past assures that the needs, vision, and contributions of older neighbors are valued and not lost; similarly, it helps to assure the healthy, successful assimilation of new neighbors. It is that shared ownership between neighbors—old and new—which nourishes the sort of neighborhood culture essential for creating positive outcomes.

The Grand Forks Community Land Trust (GFCLT) is an active partner in honoring the city's past and helping to build its future. Consistent with those goals it sponsored this neighborhood history in tandem with the building of its first home. In collaboration with University of North Dakota history professors William Caraher and Cynthia Prescott, the GFCLT has taken the steps to preserve the memory of the wood-frame church building at 224 Walnut Street.

Chris Price, a graduate student in UND's history department was enlisted to write the history you are now holding. *The Old Church on Walnut Street: A Story of Immigrants and Evangelicals*, provides a general context of Grand Forks' early history with an emphasis on its physical and cultural development. He focuses on one of the city's earliest church buildings and the two congregations that worshipped there. It is both homage to a building that served Grand Forks for nearly a century, and an invitation to embrace the ever-changing nature of all neighborhoods.

Utilizing various archival materials, Price's history considers the array of immigrants who came to North Dakota in the latter decades of the 19th century, the religious landscape in early Grand Forks, and the divisions between the city's Norwegian Lutherans who eventually came together to form United Lutheran. It is a story of people striving to preserve their culture while seeking to assimilate to their new home. Then, in the aftermath of WWI, the members of a uniquely American religion, a Church of God congregation purchased the building. Their victories and challenges ranged from a nearly devastating fire in 1944 to the joys of the 'living Christmas' tree.

The building was retired after the flood of 1997, and was eventually gifted by the city to help with the work of the city's new Community Land Trust. We hope that you enjoy this look at the physical, cultural, and religious history of Grand Forks' Near South Side neighborhood.

ACKNOWLEDGEMENTS

Like just about any endeavor that is undertaken in a professional environment, this short work did not come about through the work of any one individual. Many people have contributed to making this book a reality. Curt Hanson, Mike Swanson, and Brian Baier make up the staff at the Elwyn B. Robinson Department of Special Collections at the Chester Fritz Library on the campus of the University of North Dakota, and they were especially helpful in locating materials that have benefitted this study. Peg O'Leary with the Grand Forks Historic Preservation Commission provided important information on the old Trinity Lutheran Church building. The architectural firm of Bobbi Hepper-Olson graciously embraced the opportunity to provide professional architectural drawings.

Thanks are also in order to the Cyprus Research Fund and the Grand Forks Community Land Trust and their donors for the support they provided for this project. Bret Weber and Emily Wright were important liaisons with the Community Land Trust. Grand Forks resident Bob Glinski provided contact information for a couple of long-time members of the Grand Forks Church of God. Thomas Martzall, a member who held multiple offices in the Church of God, was kind enough to grant me a personal interview, and Wilferd Felchle allowed the use of primary documents and photographs that were indispensable in the writing the portion of this book related to the Grand Forks Church of God. Pastor Peter Coen-Tuff provided access to the historical documents of United Lutheran Church, which is the successor of Trinity Lutheran. Finally, I wish to thank UND professors William Caraher, Cynthia Prescott, and Bret Weber for their critical reading of the original manuscript and its subsequent revisions. Their inx

sightful comments improved the content and organization of this work immensely. Any remaining errors are, of course, my own. I hope that those who come across this short book enjoy reading about this portion of Grand Forks history as much as I have enjoyed writing it.

Chris Price, Grand Forks, ND

INTRODUCTION

In early March 1944 World War II raged in Europe and the Pacific, and accounts from the front lines and the home front dominated the pages of the *Grand Forks Herald*. A late winter blizzard swept through the Northern Great Plains, and the paper maintained a daily update on road conditions as North Dakotans dug their way out of the snow. Along with these headlines, the March 10 edition included a picture and caption that recorded smoke billowing from the Grand Forks Church of God as firemen worked to contain the flames (Fig. 1).[7] The building at 224 Walnut Street sustained extensive damage, but the church, undaunted, decided to repair the structure, which remained in service for the congregation until after the Grand Forks flood of 1997. The flood accomplished what the 1944 fire did not. Citing an unsound structure, the City of Grand Forks scheduled the old building for demolition in early 2012.

The old Trinity Lutheran Church, built around 1905,[8] was not terribly unique in design. Although it was the last of the wood-framed churches in downtown Grand Forks, many similar wood-framed church buildings continue to dot much of the American landscape, hearkening back to an idyllic time in the nation's history. Trinity Lutheran was not an imposing landmark on the city streetscape. The church tended to blend in with the surrounding homes in the neighborhood, and the simplicity of the structure was very much in line with that of its congregation. It was not the oldest church in town. St. Michael's Roman Catholic Church has expanded over time, but it still resides at the same lot it occupied in the early 1880s and the congregation it serves is the oldest in town. However, Trinity Lutheran and the two assemblies that worshipped within its walls were an important link to local and national history. The church at 224 Walnut Street was a tangible reminder of the immigrant struggles of early settlers on the Northern Plains as they attempted to integrate into their new homeland. This connection to early Norwegian settlers made the building important to Grand Forks history.

Just after the turn of the twentieth century, a group of Norwegian Lutherans built a new wood-framed structure on the corner of Seventh Avenue (currently Third Avenue, South) and Walnut Street in Grand Forks. While the congregation would only inhabit the building until 1918, this period in the history of the church saw the gradual assimilation of these recent immigrants into American life. This Americanization did not come without controversy, as it caused a church split and corresponded with a general drive toward Americanization that made up part of the backdrop to the fighting of World War I. The end of differences between competing Norwegian synods in 1917 paved the way for the new, unified congregation, aptly named United Lutheran. With this melding together of three Lutheran churches with Norwegian ties, Trinity Lutheran's building became expendable, and the newly unified church sold the property to the relatively new Church of God. Unlike the Lutheran Church, which had distinctly Old World roots, the Church of God was an American movement that arose out of the Holiness movement of the Second Great Awakening.

Even after its sale and transition to the Church of God congregation, for a time, the old Trinity Lutheran building at 224 Walnut Street continued its importance to Norwegian immigrants in Grand Forks who were in the process of Americanization. An early pastor, Thomas Nelson, ran the Church of God's Norwegian printing operations out of the second floor of the Grand Forks Steam Laundry on Demers Avenue (Fig. 2). One of the first pastors of the church after its move into the new building, S. O. Susag, was himself a Norwegian immigrant who preached using the Norwegian language in camp meetings that recalled the fervor of the Second Great Awakening. As Trinity Lutheran, the church functioned as the spiritual home for recent Norwegian immigrants and served as a tie to the old country; as the Grand Forks Church of God, after its early ties to the immigrant community, the church came to function as the spiritual home of a group tied to the camp meetings and the spread of evangelical religion that arose out of the nineteenth-century Second Great Awakening. The fire of 1944 nearly destroyed the structure, but the Church of God congregation rebuilt and made improvements to the building as they continued their work in the community. Then, in 1997 the floodwaters changed everything. These threads make the story of the old Trinity Lutheran Church worth remembering in the greater history of Grand Forks.

Tracing the story of this historic church, the current study begins with an overview of the early settlement of North Dakota and the Northern Great Plains. It then discusses the early religious landscape in Grand Forks, with a particular emphasis on Norwegian Lutheran activity and the controversy that American assimilation posed. The work will end by recounting the history of the Grand Forks Church of God. This congregation had its own deep ties to early Norwegian immigrants, as well as the Holiness movement that arose out of the Second Great Awakening. Both congregations were from a low church[9] background that minimized the importance of ornate buildings and ritualistic liturgies. The structure fit the personality of the Trinity congregation, as well as its successor, the Grand Forks Church of God. Such church buildings are becoming less common in urban areas, and with their disappearance, the memory of an important era in American history is in danger of being lost. This work attempts to preserve a part of that history for the Grand Forks community.

## 1. IMMIGRANTS IN EARLY NORTH DAKOTA HISTORY

This story involves an intersection between American immigration and religious history. North Dakota had the largest immigrant community per capita in the United States around the turn of the twentieth century. The 1900 census showed that more than 35 percent of North Dakota's population had been born abroad. The closest state when it came to foreign-born residents was Rhode Island, with 31 percent of its population in 1900 coming from foreign nations. Among the largest immigrant groups in North Dakota were Norwegians, Germans, and German Russians. As Norwegians and other immigrants came to North America, they attempted to maintain some semblance of a connection to their mother country while adapting to their new surroundings.[10]

Many historians have studied such migrations extensively. One of the important early works on immigration history was Oscar Handlin's *The Uprooted*, which argued that immigration altered both America and the immigrants themselves. Handlin posited, "The immigrants lived in crisis because they were uprooted. In transplantation, while the old roots were sundered, before the new were established, the immigrants existed in an extreme situation." To compensate for this feeling of uprootedness, immigrants attempted to maintain ties to Old World traditions. Handlin emphasized the religious life of these transplants, contending that the more extreme the change in life for immigrants, the more they held onto their native religious practices. State churches held a place of universality that provided a sense of belonging, and religion provided a "refuge from the anguish of the world" through a tie to the peasant's previous "day-to-day existence." The hope of the next life provided consolation to these immigrants as they took up their new lives

in a new land. Without the government providing funds for
their churches as they had become accustomed to in Europe,
these newcomers dug deeply into their own pockets to buy
existing buildings or to build new ones to house their worship.[11]

Charles Hirschman agreed with much of Handlin's thesis
regarding the religious life of immigrants. He pointed out that
assimilation in a new nation is always partial and that the process can take decades. Hirschman maintained that a "normal
feeling of loss experienced by immigrants [meant] that the familiar religious rituals learned in childhood, such as hearing
prayers in one's native tongue, [provided] an emotional connection, especially when shared with others."[12] Norwegians in
Grand Forks exhibited this immigrant pattern by building
churches within a decade of the town's founding and by utilizing Norwegian in their worship. Trinity Lutheran fit firmly into
this larger rubric, and as these immigrants continued their ethnic religious life, their building was a home that no doubt
aroused memories of their experiences in Norway.

Around the beginning of the twentieth century, Americanization became a goal that many Anglo-Americans had for new
arrivals who came from ethnic backgrounds other than their
own. President Theodore Roosevelt was one of the major ad-
vocates of using the English language as a tool to assimilate
immigrants into American society. He opposed what he viewed
as divided allegiances and wanted hyphenated Americans (i.e.,
Norwegian-Americans, Italian-Americans, etc.) to show their
complete loyalty to the United States.[13] In a work on immigration and language, Nancy C. Carnevale pointed out that for
much of early American history, English speakers generally
tolerated the speaking of foreign languages by immigrants. Although Italians were the main ethnicity that she studied,
Carnevale listed some statistics related to nineteenth-century
German-Americans. German immigrants tended to educate
their children in private and religious schools that utilized
German as a language of instruction, either exclusively or in
conjunction with English. About 180,000 children of German

ancestry studied in these schools as late as 1886. Early Norwegian pastors followed this pattern in what would become North Dakota, as they started Lutheran schools for the children of their parishioners. The Great War and calls for 100% "Americanism" (which included an ability to speak English) ended the last vestiges of this tolerance in American society.[14] It is perhaps not coincidental that the various Norwegian Lutheran churches united just after the war and that the Norwegian churches in Grand Forks switched to English in short order after the war.

The Homestead Act was a major impetus to the settlement of what would soon become North Dakota, and it was this legislation that facilitated the move of many immigrants into the new territory. By 1862, the secession of the Southern states made possible the passage of this legislation that promised to add more states in the Northern Plains. The Homestead Act made public lands available for settlement with few restrictions. The basic stipulations of the law provided that any person who was the head of a family and above twenty-one years of age could file a claim on a 160-acre plot of land. As long as the claimant improved (i.e., cultivated) the land and lived on it for five years, he (or his wife or children upon his demise) would receive a clear title to the land. Individuals could also obtain title after a six-month residency and the payment of $1.25 an acre. Many people from the eastern United States, as well as many from foreign countries, found this to be an offer they could not refuse, and they packed up their belongings to claim the nearly-free land.[15]

Eminent North Dakota historian Elwyn B. Robinson wrote of "the Great Dakota Boom" that resulted from an increasingly industrialized and urbanized American society. Railroad expansion increasingly connected isolated producers with urban markets during this period. While the Homestead Act and other similar land offers drew people to North Dakota, Robinson argued that greater industrialization and railroad building "increased both the extent and rate of western settlement, so that it moved forward in a series of booms. It was during the period of rapid industrialization in the 1880's that the Great Dakota Boom took place."[16]

In the early days of what would become North Dakota, immigrants were not the only people moving into the new territory. What began as a trickle soon became a flood of migrants, both foreign and domestic. The late nineteenth and early twentieth centuries saw a massive influx of people to the Dakota Territory, and later, the states of North Dakota and South Dakota. The 1870 census counted a mere 2,405 residents in the counties that would later constitute the state of North Dakota, although this number did not include "Indians not taxed" as stipulated in the United States Constitution. By 1900, the population had grown to 319,146. North Dakota claimed 646,872 residents in the 1920 census. The greatest growth occurred within a thirty-year period—1880 to 1910—in which the official population of the state increased by just over 540,000. The decennial censuses since 1920 have shown very little variation, and the total state population increased by less than 7,000 over a ninety-year span.[17]

Many of those who immigrated into the area during the territorial era and the early days of statehood hailed from foreign nations. The 1890 census—which was the first census after North Dakota achieved statehood—showed that nearly 45 percent of the inhabitants in the state came from other nations. Grand Forks County had similar numbers with 43.4 percent of the county's population being foreign-born in 1890. By 1900, the percentage of foreign-born residents in North Dakota indicated a decrease from the 1890 census, with just over 35 percent of North Dakota's population having been born outside the United States. The foreign-born population of Grand Forks County nearly mirrored the foreign-born population of North Dakota as a whole, with slightly fewer than 35 percent of its residents having been born abroad. The leading nations of origin among North Dakotans in 1900 (other than the United States and Canada) were Germany, Russia, and Norway. While Grand Forks County included each of these ethnic groups, Norwegians outnumbered Germans and Russians by a wide margin. In the early days of organized settlement, Norwegians congregated in the Red River Valley, with their largest concentrations located in Grand Forks, Traill, and Cass counties. The Norwegian immigrants would be influential in the early Lutheran communities in the growing town of Grand Forks. In spite of an increasing native-born population, Grand Forks County still included sizable Old World communities by 1920, although immigrants comprised only 21 percent of the county's population by that date.[18] Today, North Dakota is well below the national average in relation to its foreign-born population. Only 2.3 percent of the state is currently foreign born, compared to 12.4 percent of the population nationwide.[19]

The reasons foreign immigrants came to the Northern Great Plains often varied based upon individual circumstances. Some people came to escape persecution, while others simply came for the free land. Many immigrants to North Dakota held to Catholic or Lutheran versions of the Christian faith, but, although these faith traditions predominated, they were by no means alone on the prairie. Jewish families came from Old World nations such as Russia and Poland, often in flight from pogroms that threated life, liberty, and property. Sophie Trupin recounted her life as a Jew on the North Dakota prairie. Trupin's father, Harry Turnoy, decided to leave Russia for America after a drunken mob broke into a Sabbath meeting at his synagogue. After meeting up with a brother who previously "escaped" to Chicago in an attempt to avoid conscription into the Czar's army, Turnoy chose a quarter section in order to "win the respect of the Christian world" by working the land, rather than playing to the stereotype that viewed Jews as greedy merchants. It is estimated that "above twenty thousand" Jews came to the Dakotas and Minnesota to escape persecution between the 1880s and 1920s.[20]

Many Germans from Russia also came to North Dakota in the face of persecution. Beginning in the mid-eighteenth century, thousands of German-speaking peoples began leaving for land in the Volga and Black Sea regions of Russia at the invitation of rulers such as Catherine the Great. These Germans held varying religious beliefs, but maintained their traditional German language and culture in isolated communities. Although they were very successful farmers, later Russian czars began an attempt to assimilate the German Russians into the larger Russian state. Alexander II began the conscription of Germans in Russia, and Alexander III began a program of Russification in the 1880s. These developments led many to leave just over one hundred years after their families began flooding into Russia. Many of these families came to the Great Plains states with the promise of cheap farmland.[21]

One of the largest and most important ethnic groups to immigrate to North Dakota was the Norwegians, and it is this group that is the object of much of this study. By the end of the Great Dakota Boom, 25,773 Norwegians lived in the state. This was the largest foreign ethnicity to immigrate to North Dakota by 1890, and the Norwegian community was nearly three times larger than any other immigrant group, excluding those coming from other U.S. states and Canada. Many of these immigrants did not come directly from their motherlands, but rather from other states. One of the major starting points for these Norwegians was southern Minnesota.[22]

Norwegians often left for America because of the rampant social inequality and unrequited nationalism in Norway. In the nineteenth century, Norway broke from its centuries-old union with Denmark. The Danes controlled this relationship, with the seat of government residing in Copenhagen. In 1814, the Norwegians wrote a new constitution, and although this constitution officially considered Norway an independent nation, European powerbrokers forced Norway and Sweden to unite under a single monarch seated in Stockholm. Many Norwegians became frustrated with a class of officials who still spoke Danish, and political struggle ensued. Hans Nielsen Hauge, a lay preacher, led a revolt against the established order in the early nineteenth century, and many Norwegians began to leave their homeland. While the first boatload of these Scandinavian émigrés crossed the Atlantic on the *Restaurationen* and reached

New York in 1825, the majority of Norwegian immigrants arrived in the immediate post-Civil War era (1866-1874), the 1880s, and "the first few years of the twentieth century."[23] Trinity Lutheran began as a work tied to these later Haugean[24] migrants.

As these immigrant groups migrated to the United States in the late nineteenth and early twentieth centuries, they attempted to maintain some level of continuity with their previous lives in the Old World. Religion was one of the major areas of life that immigrants held dearly as they started life in a new land. Most often, congregations either rented space or built small wood-framed structures much like the small Trinity Lutheran church to hold their meetings. They then moved to a larger and sturdier structure if they were successful in achieving sufficient numerical and financial growth. A recent study of Catholic churches in rural areas of the Dakotas corroborates this assessment. This investigation pointed out that mission parishes quickly erected rather spartan accommodations such as a "makeshift building" in Richardton "that shook badly in the wind" or the structure constructed in an area known as Tiraspol (near Strasburg) in 1892 for $1,200. The congregants literally moved the latter structure into Strasburg when they learned that the railroad would bypass Tiraspol for Strasburg. As these parishes grew, they looked to re-create the Romanesque and Gothic Revival architecture that they associated with their former homes and built larger churches that mimicked these styles. Authors James Coomber and Sheldon Green argued:

> The immigrants who built these churches wanted to be reminded of their Old World homes; they wanted to regain the sense of community they had lost in coming here; they wanted to demonstrate their abiding faith in the future. Perhaps the urge for beauty, as seen in these churches, is in part a response by the immigrants to the lonely plains, cold winters, and life-and-death situations they found themselves in as they es-

tablished homesteads and new towns. Whatever their motivation, in building such imposing and artistic structures, early settlers were making deliberate public statements about what they felt was important.

The activities exhibited by congregations in the town of Grand Forks followed this pattern described by Coomber and Green.[25] Trinity Lutheran, in its absorption into United Lutheran, was fairly common in this regard. The church abandoned its small wood-framed structure for a larger, more modern brick building. Initially, however, their simple structure, complete with a vaguely Gothic steeple and arched windows, bespoke the congregation's connection to its background in the Haugean movement.

## 2. The Early Grand Forks Religious Landscape

To truly understand the growth of an urban area, it is important to understand its changing landscape. University of North Dakota student Alexander Aas included a crude map of Grand Forks as it looked in 1871 in his 1920 master's thesis (Fig. 3). While obviously not drawn to any scale, the general vicinity of a mere eleven structures was evident at that early date.[26] As the city grew, so did the variety of structures utilized by the population. Delores Hayden observed that "[d]wellings are the basic, repeated units in an urban neighborhood...dwellings cluster along with related buildings...that can be researched through sources such as fire insurance maps and institutional records...as well as information on individual buildings."[27] Early maps of Grand Forks tend to corroborate Hayden's assertion. New church buildings radiated outside of the downtown area as the population grew and expanded the town's boundaries.

The foundation of Grand Forks goes back to the winter of 1870-1871, when a flatboat captained by Captain Alexander Griggs mistimed the onset of winter and an early freeze caught the captain and his crew. Regarding the early days of the town, Elwyn Robinson wrote that by 1872, "Grand Forks had a boardinghouse, a hotel, a steamboat warehouse, three saloons, a stage station, a sawmill, and seven residences."[28] Contributing to the growth of the town was the completion of the Northern Pacific Railroad to Fargo. Trade between St. Paul, Minnesota, and Winnipeg (which had become part of Manitoba in 1870) was quite brisk in the post-Civil War era. An overland trail linked the Red River Valley and ran through what would become the town of Grand Forks. Owing to the volume of trade in the area and the new railroad to the south, Grand Forks became a stop on a new stage line that ran from Moorhead, Minnesota, to Winnipeg in Canada.[29]

Many people began migrating into the Red River Valley after the opening of the Dakota Territory to homesteaders. Further development followed the coming of the railroad, and religious organizations followed closely behind to minister in the new communities that sprang up on the prairie. One way to track the entrance of new religious groups into the town of Grand Forks (or other communities) is through a study of insurance maps. The Sanborn Map Company produced several fire insurance maps that detailed the landscape of Grand Forks beginning as early as 1884 (Fig. 4). These maps indicate change over time as the town's streetscape expanded over the previously open prairie. The maps also give an estimate of Grand Forks' population in intervals that do not necessarily correspond to decennial censuses, so it is possible to track growth in both the number of buildings and streets, as well as the estimated population. These maps are particularly useful in ascertaining the relative wealth and importance attached to specific buildings. Sanborn color coded structures on the maps to indicate the particular building materials used in construction. Most buildings on the Sanborn maps of Grand Forks had the designation of "dwelling" and exhibited a basic frame construction.

The Sanborn maps also indicated other buildings, such as businesses and churches. The 1884 map recorded only five church buildings in town, although some of the street names may seem unfamiliar to current Grand Fork residents: the Methodist Episcopal Church at 722 North 4th Street, the Presbyterian Church at 817 South 5th Street, the Baptist Church at 815 Alpha Avenue (currently 1st Avenue, North), St. Paul's Episcopal Church at 314 North 5th Street, and St. Michael's Catholic Church at 101 North 6th Street. The street names changed to the current configuration in the 1920s. Each of the denominations recorded in 1884 were major nation-wide organizations. However, one important point that is evident from a perusal of the map is the building materials that the churches used in their respective buildings. All of the buildings at this early date utilized a wood frame in construction, although the Presbyterians, Episcopalians, and Catholics had improved the aesthetics of their structures with a brick veneer.[30] The use of wood in early constructions conformed to the method commonly utilized in new communities, but the brick improvements served to set the churches apart from most other buildings on the city landscape.

If at first congregations built simple frame structures to house their early meetings, as these religious bodies grew along with their collective economic power, they tended to build larger structures while utilizing sturdier building materials that presented less of a fire hazard. A view of the 1888 fire insurance maps from Grand Forks bears out this point. The Baptist Church built a larger brick structure with a wood addition, while the Presbyterians and Methodists also built additions to their structures. By September 1892, all of the original congregations had at a minimum a brick-veneered church building. In addition to the five churches that remained from July 1884, four additional assemblies appeared on Grand Forks maps by 1892. According to the Sanborn maps, the additional churches were Plymouth Congregational, a "Norwegian Church," Houges (Hauge) Scandinavian Lutheran Church, and Zion Lutheran. Each of the newer groups utilized wood structures. The Scandinavian Lutheran Church was the original Trinity Lutheran congregation that would later move to 224 Walnut Street. While the Sanborn maps indicate fixed structures, they do not necessarily capture all religious activity that occurred in town for the period under consideration.[31] Some religious bodies met in buildings they did not own. For example, in December 1885, "Mr. Blanchard" of the English-speaking First Baptist Church "presented a request asking the use of [the] chapel Sunday afternoons for [a] German preaching service." The Baptists approved Blanchard's request to have their German-speaking brethren use their chapel, although how long the Germans continued to use this building is unclear because the church's official minutes say little else until the church's advisory board recommended starting a German mission in Grand Forks at a business meeting on 30 June 1908.[32] Another example is a "German Church" that met in the Montreal Hotel, as indicated by an 1888 Sanborn map.[33] At a very early date, the religious landscape in Grand Forks was quite diverse, both in the number of denominations present and the ethnic groups that these churches served.

Just a few years after the founding of town, several churches began work in Grand Forks. Some had prospered and built new and relatively ornate buildings to house their worship, while others were just beginning their work. These newer congregations tended to worship in buildings much like the one that a group of Norwegian Lutherans would build on Walnut Street in the opening years of the twentieth century.

## 3. Early Lutheran Activity in Grand Forks

The history of the Walnut Street church is incomplete without some understanding of the various groupings of Lutheran immigrants who maintained Norwegian ways after their arrival in North Dakota, for it was one of these Lutheran congregations that would both build and sell the Walnut Street church. One of the largest religious bodies throughout the history of Grand Forks has been the Lutherans. Although the earliest maps of the town indicate little activity by Lutherans, many immigrants who came to the United States in the decades immediately before and after 1900 belonged to Lutheran state churches in the Old World. Among them were Germans, Icelanders, Danes, Finns, and Norwegians. Most of these recent arrivals continued to speak their language, and felt that the continued use of their European tongues was essential for their faith.[34] The earliest Norwegians to immigrate to North Dakota fell into this pattern. They intended to continue their Lutheran faith, while using their Norwegian vernacular in their new homeland. In fact, many literally practiced their faith in their homes in the time between their arrival and the building of the first churches in their respective communities.[35] The memoir of Aagot Raaen, herself an American-born daughter of Norwegian immigrants, discussed some of the privations that many of the early settlers on the North Dakota prairies had to endure in relation to material wealth. Her own mother Ragnhild never learned either written or spoken English. These immigrants spoke Norwegian at home, in their communities, and in their churches, and many of these churches continued to use Norwegian in their services until well into the post-World War I period. Only the gradual Americanization of succeeding generations led to the transition from Norwegian to English in these churches. It is very likely that the move toward Americanization emphasized by nativist groups contributed to this shift at that particular time. This "transition was painful for the older members, and the church recognized that the shift to English was the final step in the loss of Norwegian traditions."[36] In Grand Forks, this transition would take over fifty years to accomplish completely.

By 1889, the relatively small town of Grand Forks, numbering less than 5,000 in total population,[37] had three separate Lutheran congregations with Norwegian antecedents. The first of these congregations was the Zion First Evangelical Norwegian Lutheran Church, which organized in 1879. The second of the Norwegian Lutheran assemblies in town originally went by the name of the Evangelical Lutheran Church, and began holding services in 1886. The third body originated in a split from the original Zion body in 1889 over the use of English in the church.[38] These churches would merge during the interwar years as doctrinal and liturgical practices became less of an obstacle. This merger would facilitate the sale of the Trinity Lutheran building to the Grand Forks Church of God. To understand how this merger came about, it is important to understand some of the differences that separated the various Lutheran synods in the early days of North Dakota history.

Missionary Ole Hermundsen Aaberg, himself a Norwegian immigrant, started Zion Lutheran, the first Norwegian Lutheran work in Grand Forks. Aaberg "organized at least six congregations and served eleven parishes" in various locales between 1879 and 1883, which no doubt kept him quite busy. During these years, he traveled extensively throughout the northeastern part of what would become North Dakota just a few years later. In addition to his pastoral work, Aaberg also had a hand in Lutheran educational ventures. Norwegian Lutherans founded several secondary schools in the Midwest, and Aaberg started one of these academies in Devil's Lake, North Dakota, in 1888. The school remained in operation for "about a dozen years."[39] It is apparent from these activities that Aaberg was quite important in early Lutheran work in North Dakota.

Despite its origin as a mission, Zion was able to call its first pastor, Fingar Jergenson, by 1882. Zion, in addition to being the first Lutheran church founded in town in 1879, was also the first Lutheran church in town to construct its own building in 1881 "on land purchased from Halvor and Bertha Tharaldson for the price of $538." That first building was originally very spartan in regard to its amenities, having only a dirt floor and plank pews. In spite of the cold North Dakota winters, this first church building originally had no heating system. "Mr. Oscar Larson and some others purchased a wood box stove and had it installed in the church," and the congregation expanded the structure and erected a bell tower at a cost of $800 in the early years of its existence.[40]

In 1886, a mere seven years after the founding of Zion, another itinerant preacher came into Grand Forks to begin another Norwegian congregation. It is this congregation that would become Trinity Lutheran—the very congregation that would inhabit the building on Walnut Street. Bersvend Anderson, a church planter who organized sixteen separate congregations over an eighteen-year span, began this work in Grand Forks at age sixty-five. Anderson had been a lay preacher in Norway and settled in Crookston, Minnesota, around 1876. After his ordination by the Hague Synod, he traveled extensively by foot to organize congregations in the region. Recalling Anderson's devotion, one congregant discussed how the minister walked in poor conditions:

> One year there was an exceptionally wet spring. On section #23, the land was submerged making a lake one mile long and a quarter of a mile wide. Rev. Bersvend Anderson came laboriously working his way through the mud which clung in loads to his feet. He was carrying his pack strapped on his back, as he always did on his regular trips through the country. I met him as he was trying to find a favorable place to cross this submerged bottom. He asked me if I thought the people would be able to attend his meet-

ing due to the bad roads. I asked him how he expected to get across, but he said that had never occurred to him, he was used to it. He held services in the houses as the Haugeans used to do in Norway, and after the meeting discussions followed and the host usually served lunch.[41]

Anderson and his kind were the type who with serious devotion to their cause built some of the early Lutheran churches in North Dakota. Trinity Lutheran was one of the many early churches to arise out of this effort.

Although originally named the Evangelical Lutheran Church, this second congregation founded by Bersvend Anderson came to be known as the Trinity Lutheran Church in short order.[42] The church first appeared on insurance maps in 1892 as the Houges (which was a mistaken spelling for Hauge) Scandinavian Lutheran Church, and this appellation remained in 1897. By January 1901, the congregation was known as the Trefoldigheds (Norwegian for Trinity) Scandinavian Lutheran Church. The original building that the church utilized sat at 11 Walnut Street. In the first decade of the twentieth century, however, the church moved to the corner of 3rd Avenue and Walnut Street, and came to occupy 224 Walnut Street, which was a lot that set diagonally across from the home of the Zion Lutheran congregation at 24 Chestnut Street (currently 324 Chestnut Street).[43] Although both of these congregations claimed Lutheran heritage, they belonged to different synods. For decades, these competing synods did not have terribly good relations.

Early Lutherans who immigrated to America set up synods according to their ethnic heritage and theological position. Doctrinal differences caused the initial division between Lutheran congregations in Grand Forks. Both Zion and Trinity utilized Norwegian, so linguistic considerations did not dictate their remaining separate congregations. The reason for the initial division related to doctrine and practice. Before 1917, Norwegian Lutherans in the United States belonged to three separate synods: the Hauge's Norwegian Evangelical Lutheran

Synod in America, the Norwegian Synod, and the United Norwegian Lutheran Church in America.[44]

The Hauge Synod had its origins in the teachings of Hans Nielsen Hauge, a lay evangelist in early nineteenth-century Norway. While Hauge never left the official state church of Norway, he nonetheless aroused suspicion among authorities in his homeland. Hauge's ministry achieved its popularity as a reaction against an increasing rationalism in the Norwegian state church. The University of Copenhagen prepared ministers for Norwegian churches and saw a rise in Enlightenment thinking during the late 1700s and early 1800s. In spite of this rationalism, most Norwegian pastors remained fairly orthodox in their teachings. Hauge, in contrast to a rational orthodoxy, emphasized Christian experience of a more pietistic sort, adherence to the Old Testament law, and repentance. His teaching led to several arrests for breaking the Conventicle Act of 1741 that prohibited itinerant lay preaching. In spite of official opposition to his work, his teachings found fertile ground in the lives of many Norwegians, some of whom immigrated to the United States.[45] The Haugeans in America organized into the Eielsen and Hauge Synods, neither of which was terribly large. However, Lutheran historians E. Clifford Nelson and Eugene L. Fevold argued that "by the seventies of the nineteenth century Haugeans had found their way into all the church bodies."[46] It was to this group that Trinity Lutheran belonged.

The Norwegian Synod was a much larger body in the early twentieth century. This organization opposed views that challenged formal worship, such as those held by Eielsen and other Haugeans, and preferred rather a "theological orthodoxism bordering on uncharitableness and churchly order clinging firmly to traditional practices."[47] The Norwegian Synod held to a conservative traditionalism, while the Hauge Synod preferred a more liberal pietistic faith.[48] The United Lutherans fell between these groups after their organization as a union of three smaller bodies in 1890.[49] A 1900 census of Lutheran bodies in the United States found that the United Lutheran Synod had approximately 130,000 congregants in 1,121 congregations, which were served by 361 pastors. The same census showed the Norwegian Synod to have 252 ministers serving 739 churches with 66,927 members. The Hauge Synod, the group with which Trinity Lutheran was affiliated, was the smallest of the three groups with 12,540 worshipers in 212 congregations. Ninety-five ministers conducted services in Hauge Synod churches.[50]

In the early twentieth century, University of North Dakota student Anders Hillesland interviewed several individuals for his thesis on Norwegian Lutherans in the Red River Valley. An interview with a Mr. Jacobson indicates "the religious conditions of the time":

> When I came from Iowa I could not understand why, on Sundays, my boss…drove past the little frame church near his home, and attended services in the big stone church farther down the road. He told me that the congregation and pastor of the big stone church were Synod people and the other were Hauges. I attended both and saw little difference except in the ceremonies which in the former were similar to those used in Norway, while in the other everything was informal.[51]

This account indicates clearly the differences in both the liturgy and buildings utilized by the two synods and shows how outsiders might have viewed the Haugeans.

Just after Trinity Lutheran's establishment as the second Lutheran church in town in January 1886, it built its first building on the one hundred block of Walnut Street in 1887. The cost of this initial building was $3,000, which would amount to approximately $78,100 in 2016 currency when taking simple inflation into account. In 1892 the church built an addition to the original building at a cost of $600, and in 1900 the congregation built a *prestehus* (rectory) for $3,500 ($103,000 in 2016 dollars).[52] With a dearth of trained ministers, it was not unusual for multiple assemblies to share clerics. This made for extensive travel for these circuit riders. M. G. Hanson, who served as Trinity Lutheran's third pastor from 1892-1898, estimated that he rode about 2,300 miles on horseback and 7,087 miles by rail during his tenure at the church. These pastors did not undertake their work with an eye toward riches. Salaries ranged from $100 to $300 annually for Lutheran ministers in Grand Forks, although noncash gifts were not uncommon. Trinity "offered a visiting pastor $5 per service plus collection" in 1893. The church set compensation in 1913 for its priest, N. S. Lohre, at $300 plus use of the parsonage and three special offerings.[53] This paltry salary would amount to approximately $7,500 in 2016 based upon a simple accounting for inflation. These poor salaries were much less than a church might pay a full-time pastor. For example, J. F. Mills, the pastor of First Baptist Church received a three-month vacation from his congregation to "take a trip to Palestine and the Orient."[54] It is highly unlikely that the pastors of this small Lutheran congregation would have had the funds to take such a trip on their small salaries. In the first decade of the twentieth century, Trinity Lutheran moved to the building at 224 Walnut Street, where it would remain until its merger into what would become United Lutheran Church in 1918.[55]

The third of the early Lutheran churches in Grand Forks with a tie to Norway was the curiously named First Lutheran Church. This assembly resulted from the assimilation of the parishioners of Zion Lutheran into American culture. Those "who chose to become Americanized aligned themselves with the synod called the United Norwegian Lutheran Church in America." This group of Americanized Norwegians remained in Zion Lutheran. However, not all members of the Zion church cared to Americanize. Those who maintained Norwegian culture in church joined the Norwegian Evangelical Lutheran Church in America and broke off to form their own congregation in 1889. By 1893, the church took the name of First Lutheran, which was interesting considering its genesis in a church split. Most likely, the use of this name intended to hide the schism from the remembrance of posterity. First Lutheran bought a corner of the lot on which Trinity had its original church building. The small church soon moved to the corner of 2nd Avenue, South, and Cottonwood Street.[56]

The Norwegian Lutherans in Grand Forks emphasized Christian education in their churches. The membership considered the confirmation service the "fulfillment of religious education. To be confirmed one was expected to have thorough knowledge of the teaching of the church." These confirmation services could be quite long, lasting as long as five hours, and some candidates answered in both Norwegian and English. Each of the churches had Sunday Schools for instructing students. [57]

These early churches also emphasized music. Organs were a common instrument that provided accompaniment for congregational and choir singing, although these pieces of musical instrumentation were at times quite primitive. According to United Lutheran's hundred-year anniversary publication, the organs required "human endeavor" in addition to an organ player. These organs were pump organs and "[m]any times young boys were asked to work the pumps for the organ. Depending upon the mood of the boys, there would be soft or blasting notes emanating throughout the church." At times, the churches would pay organists and choir directors for their efforts. Trinity did not fall outside this norm, and in 1892, Kay Johnson earned a salary of $5 a month for her musical efforts.[58] The next year, the church "decided to rent an organ" to aid its musical program.[59] This last point is somewhat surprising, considering the general austerity of the church and its synodical ties.

An easing of the doctrinal and liturgical differences between the synods led to the eventual merger of Zion, Trinity, and First Lutheran. By the late 1880s, most Norwegian bodies, with the exception of the Hauge Synod, began favoring a union that would do away with the multiplicity of synods among Norwegian-American Lutherans. In 1889 "the respective annual synodical meetings...with the exception of Hauge's Synod, gave enthusiastic approval to the union proposals."[60]

By the early 1910s, there was hope that a complete union could be accomplished in 1917 to coincide with the 400th anniversary of the Protestant Reformation. Not surprisingly, the Hauge Synod was the biggest concern and the longest holdout. The important disputes that worried the Haugeans were ecumenism and liturgical practices, both of which they opposed. After receiving assurances that eased their concerns regarding these issues, the Hauge Synod approved three "enabling acts" and cleared the largest obstacle along the road to union.[61]

After the three synods merged during a meeting in St. Paul, Minnesota, the Norwegian Lutheran Church of America emerged according to schedule in 1917. Within a decade, the three Grand Forks churches would likewise merge. The first merger occurred in April 1918 as Zion and Trinity joined to form Bethany Lutheran. In the era of American involvement in World War I, the new church agreed that "the work of the church be carried out in English and Norwegian equally" and held services in both languages. The new assembly met in the Zion building at 324 Chestnut Street (the current site of United Lutheran Church), and held an installation service on May 26 for David Stoeve, the former pastor of Zion Lutheran. The church and the rectory on the Walnut Street property lost their usefulness to the church at this point. In 1926, First Lutheran decided to join Bethany. This show of unity among the churches with ties to Norway gave birth to United Lutheran.[62] Similar consolidations took place near in this general time frame in many North Dakota communities, including Fargo, Mayville, and Hillsboro.[63]

In 1921, First Lutheran transitioned to the exclusive use of English, which was ironic considering its birth as a congregation that splintered from another body because of a desire to maintain Norwegian culture. The gradual switch to English among the Norwegians was complete by about 1930. United Lutheran was the first church in the merged synod to utilize only English for preaching, a practice that arose out of a growing concern that English-speaking children would leave for English-speaking churches. The early Norwegian-American period of Grand Forks Lutheranism came to a close.[64] By the 1930s, United Lutheran built a new building and became the largest church in the new synod with over 5,000 members.[65] As the old churches merged into the new body, the old buildings became expendable, and Bethany Lutheran sold the old Trinity Lutheran building at 224 Walnut Street to a Church of God congregation for $5,000 in 1919.

## 4. The Church of God on Walnut Street

The history of the old Trinity Lutheran Church involved an immigrant community that adhered to an Old World state church. The history of the building also included an evangelical community rooted in the Second Great Awakening and the nineteenth-century Holiness tradition. Although the Grand Forks Church of God had important ties to this evangelical movement, its early days also included some very close ties to the Norwegian immigrant community of the Red River Valley. The church and its building experienced several setbacks throughout the twentieth century. In spite of eventually leaving the building at 224 Walnut Street, the Church of God, much like United Lutheran, continues to serve the Grand Forks community.

Renowned historian of American religion Mark Noll referred to the Second Great Awakening as "the most influential revival of Christianity in the history of the United States" that "provided a pattern and an impetus for similar waves of revival that continued...until after the Civil War." Inseparably tied to the memory of the Second Awakening is the protracted camp meeting. The most famous of these camp meetings occurred at Cane Ridge, Kentucky, in 1801, and this massive revival led to the establishment of other such assemblies that attempted to recreate its spiritual fervor. Many new churches arose out of this widespread revivalism. Some preachers from the Methodist persuasion began to emphasize John Wesley's concern for "Christian perfection," thus beginning the Holiness movement. In addition to a greater emphasis on religion and personal holiness, the Second Great Awakening also led to the establishment of several new denominations on the frontier.[66]

Nathan Hatch argued that the Second Great Awakening was a major democratizing influence in the early national period of United States history, disputing claims by earlier historians such as Perry Miller and Richard Hofstadter, who viewed this epoch in American history as "a conservative assertion of authority by ministers fearful of losing their traditional roles." The Second Awakening saw the growth of untrained, yet charismatic leaders who led a populist religious movement that democratized religion in America.[67] This democratization diminished the authority of more established denominations.

While the Holiness movement originated in Methodism, the democratization of American religion led to its expansion outside of the Methodist umbrella. This sentiment by "come-outers" intensified and led to the rise of even more Holiness denominations and movements by the 1880s. Around this time, the Church of God reformation movement became one of the groups to spin off from the Methodist Holiness movement. The theological roots of what would become the Church of God of Anderson, Indiana,[68] involved a belief in complete sanctification as a second work of grace and the sinfulness of denominations as needless divisions in the body of Christ.[69] This group continued in the tradition of the camp meetings of the Second Awakening, and began its involvement in the Grand Forks area in 1895.

The Grand Forks Church of God began activity well before its move into the former Trinity Lutheran building on 224 Walnut Street in 1919. The local congregation was (and continues to be) affiliated with the Church of God of Anderson, Indiana, which began as a movement with profound Wesleyan and Pietist influences. While generally evangelical in its doctrine, the Church of God generally denounced denominationalism and sought to transcend the various Protestant sects. The man considered most influential in the 1881 foundation of this new movement was Daniel S. Warner, who with

> several associates sought to forsake denominational hierarchies and formal creeds, trusting solely in the

Holy Spirit as their overseer and the Bible as their
statement of belief. These individuals saw themselves
at the forefront of a movement to restore unity and
holiness to the church. Their aim was not to establish
another denomination but to promote primary alle-
giance to Jesus Christ so as to transcend
denominational loyalties.

While this new movement arose out of the nineteenth-century
holiness movement, the Church of God, Anderson, did not
emphasize charismatic gifts such as speaking in tongues as did
some other holiness groups like Pentecostals.[70]

The Church of God first appeared in Grand Forks in
1895, with the arrival of traveling ministers George W. Bailey
and J. C. Peterman (Fig. 5). The mother of future Church of
God minister and college founder Albert F. Gray held a meeting in her home at 616 5th Avenue South in Grand Forks with
several individuals who wanted personal holiness. According to
Gray's autobiography, "Methodists, Baptists, Salvationists [Sal-
vation Army], Free Methodists, and a few others attended this
meeting." Bailey met with them and argued against denominational divisions from 1 Corinthians 1 and 3. The Grand Forks
Church of God that would utilize the Walnut Street property
traces its origins to these early meetings in November 1895.[71]

Shortly after these meetings, the new congregation began
meeting on the second floor of the Grand Forks Steam Laundry building on Demers Avenue. The owner of the laundry,
Charles G. Neils, was himself a devoted follower of the
Church of God. The church did not remain at this address for
long, however, and purchased a small wood-framed church
building on the corner of Cottonwood and 2nd Avenue, South,
in 1900 (Fig. 6). The church remained in this building until
1919, when it purchased the old Trinity Lutheran building upon the merger of Zion Lutheran and Trinity Lutheran.[72]

The early activities of the Church of God, prior to its
move to Walnut Street, included camp meetings, a form of
ministry that became popular in frontier evangelical circles during the period of the Second Great Awakening. This major

revival of American religious sentiments began around the turn of the nineteenth century on the campuses of early American colleges. Revivals broke out among the Presbyterians at Hampton-Sidney College and Washington College, both around 1787 in Virginia, and a northern awakening began under the preaching of President Timothy Dwight at Yale College in 1801. This northern branch of the revival then spread to Dartmouth and other colleges. While these events occurred among the educated in urban settings, the revival also spread to the frontier. In these rural areas, people began to meet in camps for lengthy meetings, such as the previously mentioned Cane Ridge meeting. From these beginnings, the camp meetings became a staple of American evangelical life up into the twentieth century.[73]

Those affiliated with Church of God teachings in North Dakota held their first camp meeting in 1896 near Arthur, about thirty miles northwest of Fargo. The camp meeting came to Grand Forks the following year, and the "Church of God Reformation," as they then referred to themselves, bought a plot near the Red River in 1899. People from many different communities traveled to the Grand Forks camp meeting in the early years, some coming from as far afield as eastern Montana and Manitoba. Each camp meeting included sermons and singing. Camp cooks and local farmers provided food for the assembled campers, and the wife of the Grand Forks pastor "always assumed the responsibility of managing the kitchen and dining area."[74]

While most of the people involved with the Church of God movement were English speakers, in Grand Forks there was also activity among German and Scandinavian immigrants.

> A large number of first-generation Germans and Scandinavians attended the meetings. In the early years each of the ethnic groups had one service a day, scheduled between the general English services. In fact the Scandinavians had two services a day for several years. In 1900 (perhaps in a few other years too) a

baptismal service was held in Norwegian, German and English. But as these groups got more and more accustomed to hearing and understanding English the special meetings for them were no longer necessary.[75]

This declining need for special ethnic services indicated a greater level of assimilation for these new Americans. In addition to these considerations given to the Scandinavian brethren, Grand Forks was also important to the overall Church of God outreach through its publication of ethnic literature. After the church moved out of the second floor of the Grand Forks Steam Laundry, the space became a center for the Norwegian version of *The Gospel Trumpet* (*Evangeliske Bason*), which was the main publication of the Church of God. The minister of the Grand Forks church, Thomas Nelson, was one of the most important Scandinavian leaders in the Church of God and ran this operation until moving to St. Paul with his publishing work in 1902 (Figs. 7 and 8).[76]

Another Scandinavian connection in the early days of the Grand Forks Church of God was Pastor S. O. Susag, who was himself born in Norway. Susag served as the pastor of the Grand Forks church from December 1919 to November 1925 and claimed to have baptized over 200 individuals during his tenure at the church. He also took part in the annual Grand Forks camp meeting. His recollections spoke to the cosmopolitan nature of these early camp meetings, as he remembered preaching in the "Scandinavian language" to the people assembled. Susag spent much of his later ministry as an itinerant speaker, but his memoirs nonetheless include several reminiscences from his time in Grand Forks.[77] This Norwegian emphasis declined over time, and the church's ethnic outreach gradually emphasized foreign mission work, rather than local cross-cultural ministries. Susag began his work with the Grand Forks Church of God shortly after his congregation moved into the Trinity Lutheran building, and his ministry marked the transition of the building from a distinctly ethnic use to one tied almost exclusively to an English-speaking congregation.

## 5. THE TRINITY LUTHERAN BUILDING AFTER THE NORWEGIANS

Though never a large church, the Grand Forks Church of God saw its largest attendance in the decade after its purchase of the old Trinity Lutheran Church, averaging around 100 in attendance for most of the 1920s. With a congregation this size, there was no need to purchase or build another structure because the old building effectively met the church's needs. The number of those attending the services declined after this era, but the church continued its activity in town. In spite of these relatively small numbers, some of the members of this church became quite influential in the Church of God movement on a national level. A member of the first graduating class of what is now known as Anderson University and the founders of two other Church of God colleges had important ties to the church in Grand Forks. Anna Koglin, author of the church's seventy-fifth anniversary history and a history of the broader Church of God movement in North Dakota, graduated from the Anderson Bible Training School, and influenced the founding of another school in Texas through her interaction with Max R. Gaulke.[78]

Max Gaulke was a second-generation North Dakotan of German descent who was born in a house at 902 Belmont Road in Grand Forks on 10 August 1902. His family was active in the local Methodist Church until his mother broke her ties and joined the Church of God movement (Fig. 9). While Bertha Gaulke took young Max with her to the Church of God meetings, the older children continued as Methodists with their father, Maximillian. Bertha Gualke herself served as pastor of the church for three short stints in the coming years. Remembering the people at his new church, Max Gaulke found them "sincere and zealous though certainly not Grand Forks aristocrats." (Figs. 10 and 11) After spending two years studying at the University of North Dakota, his brother convinced him to enroll at Anderson College, the Church of God's flagship school. In spite of his self-described sinful ways that included such transgressions as attending dances, Gaulke began studies at Anderson and shortly thereafter converted to the religion of his mother. Albert F. Gray, another Church of God minister with Grand Forks ties, baptized him. After earning a Bachelor of Divinity from Chicago Theological Seminary, he became pastor of the West Eleventh Church of God in Houston, Texas, and earned a master's degree from the University of Houston. In 1953 Gaulke started the South Texas Bible Institute with twenty-six students. He served as president of the school until his retirement in 1975. In 1985 the school, then known as Gulf Coast Bible College, moved from Houston to Oklahoma City and became Mid-America Bible College (now Mid-America Christian University). The foundation of a successful college cemented Gualke's importance in the history of the Church of God. Although he moved away from Grand Forks to serve his church on a national stage, Gaulke continued to return to his hometown annually until his death from a heart attack, ironically suffered in 1992 while driving home from one of these vacations.[79]

Albert Frederick Gray was likewise an influential Church of God minister who had ties to the Grand Forks Church of God. Gray's father died in 1887, and his family moved to Grand Forks in 1891. Gray's parents had been Baptists, and his family attended the First Baptist Church in Grand Forks until his mother became angry because the church asked the children to give a collection for a gift for R. B. Griffith, the superintendent of the church's Sunday school and owner of the quite profitable Ontario Store. Gray recalled, "Mother was disgusted that the children should be asked to buy a chair for this rich man so she said to me, 'I don't care if you never go to that Sunday school again,' so I quit going." The Gray home housed the initial meeting that gave rise to the Grand Forks

Church of God in 1895. After moving to Bottineau County, North Dakota, the family continued to return for the camp meetings in Grand Forks until their move to Spokane, Washington in 1902.[80]

Gray returned to Grand Forks on occasion. He was the featured speaker at the sixtieth anniversary service of the Grand Forks Church of God in 1955.[81] However, his importance in the Church of God related mainly to his part in the founding of Pacific Bible College (now known as Warner Pacific College) and his service in other organizational positions. Pacific Bible College opened its doors on October 5, 1937, with twenty-one students. Gray served as the president of the college and a member of the Board of Trustees for the first twenty years of the school's existence and was a member of the faculty from 1937 to 1960. Before his foundational work in the early years of Pacific Bible College, Gray taught and served as a member of the Executive Committee at Anderson College, while simultaneously serving as the minister of the Park Place Church of God in Anderson, Indiana. His work for the Church of God also included a stint as the President of the Missionary Board. In addition to his service for the Church of God movement, Gray was a frequent contributor to *The Gospel Trumpet* and also wrote four books. It would be difficult to overstate his importance for the Church of God during the mid-twentieth century.[82]

While important individuals from Grand Forks like Gray and Gaulke made their mark in the Church of God after moving away from the city, the church in Grand Forks continued its work. Unfortunately, an event in March 1944 threatened the congregation and its building. At 11:06 A. M. on the morning of March 9, 1944, the Grand Forks Fire Department responded to a call regarding the old Trinity Lutheran structure at 224 Walnut Street. Apparently, a faulty chimney connection in the pastor's study started a fire in the building. From this origin, the fire quickly spread through the frame structure, and caused heavy damage to its interior. At the time, Ralph E. Rowe, the pastor of the Grand Forks Church of God informed the *Grand*

*Forks Herald* that the "windows, roof and furniture were total losses, while contractors said that the walls, which remained standing, could be repaired."[83]

During the last two years of Ralph Rowe's pastorate (1944-1946), the church began and completed the process of rebuilding the sanctuary. Church historian Anna Koglin pointed out that the church had "little insurance coverage and the congregation was struggling through a time of drought and economic recession."[84] The small congregation continued its work of rebuilding in spite of these obstacles (Fig. 12). By the end of Rowe's pastorate, the church completed the rebuilding of the sanctuary for approximately $8,000 (which would be about $98,300 in 2016).[85]

In 1946, Ray Finley became pastor and began the job of leading the congregation and paying off the debt incurred to rebuild the church. Finley was a Grand Forks native who graduated from Central High School. After his graduation, he moved to Anderson, Indiana, to study at the Church of God's ministerial college. Due to poor health, he ended his studies and took a pastorate in Bowdon, North Dakota. He returned to Grand Forks to assume the pastorate at the Grand Forks Church of God. The church grew in numerical strength under Finley, and in May 1948, the church burned the mortgage taken out when the congregation decided to rebuild after the 1944 fire. The church was not finished improving its property, however. Under Finley's oversight, the church borrowed around $5,000 in additional funds "to construct a full concrete basement and install a good oil heating system." The congregation retired this additional debt in 1953, just a few days before the sudden death of their pastor.[86] "He died unexpectedly...at a farm near Cummings, North Dakota where they were visiting" while recovering from surgery on some stomach ulcers. Finley was only thirty-four when he passed off the scene, leaving not only the church, but also his wife and three daughters behind. After about a decade of numerous troubles beginning with the 1944 fire, the church entered a period of relative stability.[87]

Periodic renovations and improvements to the building continued over the next few years. Under the ministry of Melvin Miller in the mid-1960s, the church undertook a sizeable renovation of the basement, adding some classrooms, a second furnace, and a baptistery (Fig. 13). Pastor Joe McCraw led the congregation for a time in the 1970s and started a local bus ministry, which drew thirty-plus additional attendees to services. It was during McCraw's ministry that the church purchased a new parsonage at 2607 Cherry Street so that it could utilize the old rectory for a growing Sunday school program.[88]

The Grand Forks Church of God also involved itself in community evangelism. An undated pamphlet produced by the church attempted to introduce the group to locals who may have been unfamiliar with the congregation. This literature attempted to answer some important questions that locals may have had. Included in this brochure titled "You Are Invited to the First Church of God" was a listing of specific ministries that the church provided, such as Sunday preaching and worship, a Wednesday evening Bible study, youth activities, men's and women's groups, a nursery, and a weekly Saturday morning prayer breakfast. The church desired to make it known that it was a welcoming community that wanted to support its neighborhood. Finally, the church made clear its particular doctrinal distinctiveness for those who may have been interested. In addition to beliefs that exhibited ideas from both the evangelical and holiness movements, such as salvation by grace and victory over sin, the church proclaimed its particular understanding of the church (in a universal sense). True to its Church of God roots, the Grand Forks body distanced itself from denominational splintering and refused to follow a particular creed, other than the New Testament itself.[89]

In its later years at the Walnut Street property, one of the biggest outreaches that the church conducted involved a "singing Christmas tree." For several years before the 1997 Grand Forks flood, the First Church of God utilized this tree that was seventeen feet tall by twenty-two feet wide and which had room for a choir of fifteen singers. Long-time member Wilferd Felchle designed the tree in the mid-1980s after Debbie Tomlinson, the pastor's wife, brought the idea to his attention. The construction of the tree utilized a green-painted plywood frame and branches from several artificial trees. Wrapped around the branches were thousands of Christmas lights, controlled by eight switches. Constructing the tree each year was labor intensive and took about eighty man-hours of work. After use each holiday season, the church stored the tree in the old parsonage. In addition to the singing Christmas tree, the church once held a concert at the Columbia Mall in Grand Forks. On another occasion, Felchle remembered the church holding a live nativity scene in front of its building. "We almost froze to death. It was around 30 below." The last use of the tree for a Christmas program occurred in 1996. The next spring's massive flood would bring an end to much more than the singing Christmas tree.[90]

In April 1997, one of the worst floods in recent American history occurred when the Red River of the North overflowed into the town of Grand Forks and caused one of the largest evacuations in United States history. Among the buildings affected was the old Trinity Lutheran Church, home of the Grand Forks Church of God since 1919. Thomas Martzall, the treasurer for the Church of God in 1997, lived across the street from the church building and removed items of importance from the building before the flood hit. The floodwaters poured into the basement of the old church, nearly reaching the rafters that held up the main floor. After the flood, the church cleaned out the basement and resumed services in the building for about two months. Attendance dropped after the flood as some of the families in the church moved away, not wanting to live in a flood zone.

Shortly after the resumption of services in the old building, the City of Grand Forks offered to buy the building from the congregation. Martzall, who had served as a member of the building and grounds committee, in addition to his work as treasurer, indicated that this offer in some ways came as a blessing to the congregation. Changes in society had actually led to talk of the church moving its services before the flood. As a church built into the neighborhood in the early 1900s when most people walked extensively, parking was no problem. However, as more people began driving to church, the lack of adequate parking became a liability. Furthermore, the church built restrooms in the basement of the building before the passage of the Americans with Disabilities Act in 1990. The cost to make these facilities accessible also contributed to the talk of moving to a building that would not need such modifications. After the flood, the church took the city's offer and moved its operations to 2856 North Washington Street, where it remains to the present day. The old Trinity Lutheran structure was abandoned.[91]

CONCLUSION

In the late 1800s, a group of Scandinavian Lutheran immigrants who adhered to the teachings of Hans Nielsen Hauge banded together in Grand Forks, North Dakota, to form a church that tied them to their homeland and their doctrine. In the first decade of the twentieth century, the Trinity Lutheran Church built a new building to house its Norwegian meetings. With the unification of the competing Norwegian synods and the increasing Americanization of its parishioners, Trinity Lutheran joined with its estranged brethren in the Zion Lutheran and First Lutheran congregations. The birth of United Lutheran Church opened the building at 224 Walnut Street for a group with a distinctly American origin. The Church of God arose out of the Second Great Awakening, which did much to democratize American religion, and the Holiness movement—itself one of the democratic offshoots of the Second Awakening. The Church of God bought the old building from Trinity Lutheran for $5,000 and moved to this new location in 1919. Fire nearly consumed the small wood-framed church in 1944, but the flames failed to destroy it. What fire could not achieve, water did. While the city of Grand Forks scheduled the demolition of the old Trinity Lutheran building in early 2012, the structure that stood at the corner of 3rd and Walnut uniquely represented two important movements in American religious history. As a result of these ties to the history of Grand Forks and the United States, the building and the congregants of its two occupant churches deserve remembrance in the town's collective memory.

In 2011, the city of Grand Forks announced that the old Trinity Lutheran building would be demolished because of an unsound structure. The building had long supported the community, but its last congregation left the building, and the city purchased it after the massive flood in 1997. Ownership of the property eventually fell to the Grand Forks Community Land Trust.

Grand Forks Community Land Trust (GFCLT) is a nonprofit organization dedicated to providing quality, affordable homeownership opportunities for people who may not otherwise have the opportunity to obtain such property. The GFCLT is one of the over 250 similar land trusts that were active in 44 states as of 2011. CLTs lease the land on which the homes in their portfolio sit to reduce the cost to low and moderate income buyers who may not otherwise be able to afford their own homeownership. GFCLT homebuyers own the homes and are then able to sell them, providing an opportunity for positive equity and upward economic mobility. Homes in GFCLT's portfolio are sold based on a formula that appreciates on the original purchase price. To retain the availability of affordable homeownership opportunities, buyers are required to sell GFCLT homes to either other eligible buyers or back to the GFCLT.[92]

One of the purposes of the Grand Forks Community Land Trust is to provide stability in the community. Owners of Land Trust houses tend to remain in their homes for lengthy periods, as "in a recent study over 90% of CLT families remained in their homes for at least 5 years. Of these families, over 70% went on to purchase owner-occupied, market rate homes." Those with a financial stake in their homes are more likely to take care of the property and their communities. The boards of directors of Community Land Trusts also tend to have a stake in the success of the community as "homeowners" and "community members" each make up at least one-third of these bodies.[93]

Equally important to its commitment to providing affordable homeownership opportunities, Grand Forks Community Land Trust is also dedicated to improving the overall quality of housing in Grand Forks. The Historic Near South End, 224 Walnut's neighborhood, holds some of the most significant historic buildings in Grand Forks, yet many of its homes have fallen to disrepair or were demolished following the flood of 1997. Through the established partnerships with Grand Forks' Historic Preservation Commission, the Office of Urban Development, and the UND History Department, GFCLT plans to build homes that revive the Historic Near South End authentically to its formerly thriving state. Once work in this area has progressed, the organization plans to move to other struggling neighborhoods in the community, continually improving the overall quality of housing stock.

Those who know the area well may miss the house of worship at 224 Walnut and the old, walkable Near South End. While Grand Forks Community Land Trust cannot duplicate the spirit of this historic neighborhood, the organization will breathe new life into it by building homes on empty lots, bringing back single-family homeownership, and moving in young families with children to attend the under-populated elementary school nearby. Though the spirit will be a bit different, Grand Forks Community Land Trust's work will bring back one of the most important elements of North Dakota's historic wood-frame churches – the sense of community.

# Appendices

APPENDIX 1: PASTORS WHO SERVED TRINITY LUTHERAN OR
THE GRAND FORKS CHURCH OF GOD

## Pastors of Trinity Lutheran Church

Bersvend Anderson (1882-1886)
G. C. Gjerstad (1887-1891)
M. G. Hanson (1892-1898)
M. J. Westphal (1892-1898)
D. T. Borgen (1898-1899)
O. Andreson (1899-1909)
J. T. Krogstad (1903-1906)
G. O. Mona (1907-1912)
L. J. Odland (1909-1910)
N. J. Lohre (1912-1918)

## Pastors of the Grand Forks Church of God

George W. Bailey (1895-1897)
Charles H. Tubbs (1898-1901 and 1902-1917)
Thomas Nelson (1901-1902)
Zeno Newell (1917-1919)
Seward L. Johnson (1917-1919)
Albert G. Ahrendt (1919-1921)
S. O. Susag (1922-1924)
Bertha Gaulke (1926-1928, 1933-1936, 1938)
Arthur Mock (1929-1930)
Allison F. Barnard (1931-1932)
Paul Cook (1937)
William J. Ayotte (1939-1943)
Ralph Rowe (1943-1946)
Ray L. Finley (1946-1953)
Cecil D. Evans (1953-1964)
Melvin Miller (1964-1965)

Ray Martin (1966-1967)
Jerry S. Jones (1968-1971)
John Baird (1971-1973)
Joe McCraw (1973-1979)
Michael D. Thompson (1979-1984)
Jeffrey L. Tomlinson (1984-1988)
Randal Phillips (1988-1994)
John Beau Lac (1994)
Walter Truex (1994-1997 flood)

APPENDIX 2: ARCHITECTURAL DESCRIPTION
Aaron Barth, North Dakota State University

Trinity Lutheran Church (Site 32GF2013) is built in craftsman style, and the main portion is a cross gable design. The southwest corner has an integrated shed roof, and the southeast corner has a gothic revivalism tower, a style common with country cottages, churches and public buildings between 1830 through the 1880s. The broach tower extending up out of the southeast corner reflects additional elements of Carpenter Gothic Revivalism, this drawing from the broader gothic revivalist movement of the nineteenth century. The broach tower is an octagonal spire surmounting a square tower. Gothic revivalism emphasized this type of verticality, and in the context of the church this intended to draw the eyes upward toward the sky and presumably toward the heavens.[1]

The entire church has a concrete foundation and it is of wood frame construction. The exterior walls were originally sheathed with horizontal drop wood siding, but by 2001 it had been modernized with horizontal drop metal siding. The north elevation has four, four-light double hung windows. The east elevation has eight, four-light double hung windows, a pair of wooden entrance doors with two single-light windows, and a wood lancet arch ventilator and a rectangular ventilator. The south elevation has nine four-light double hung windows, a personnel door with one single-light deadlight window, a wood lancet arch ventilator and a rectangular ventilator. The west elevation has a two-light double hung window and a two-light sliding window. The brick chimney protrudes from the roof

---

[1] Cyril Harris, *American Architecture: An Illustrated Encyclopedia* (New York and London: W.W. Norton, 1998), 39 &154-155.

and is offset on the southwest slope. The broach tower is covered with wood shakes, and the remainder of the cross gable roof is covered with asphalt shingles.

The church was first recorded in 1981 by R. Palmer, and updated by Frank Vyzralek in 1985, and "LCT" in 1989. Harleen Young provided the first stylistic description of the church in 1995, and Andrew Peterson submitted photographic updates in 1998. Thomas Isern and Jeff Hoffer updated the site form in 2001, and noted that the church had been modified with the addition of horizontal metal siding. Flood damage from 1997 ultimately contributed to the decision in 2012 by the city of Grand Forks to demolish the church.

East Building Elevation

0      5'      10'      15'      20'

Grand Forks Lutheran Church
224 Walnut Street, Grand Forks, North Dakota
Prepared September 2011 from field measurements

HEPPER OLSON architects

North Building Elevation

0    5'    10'    15'    20'

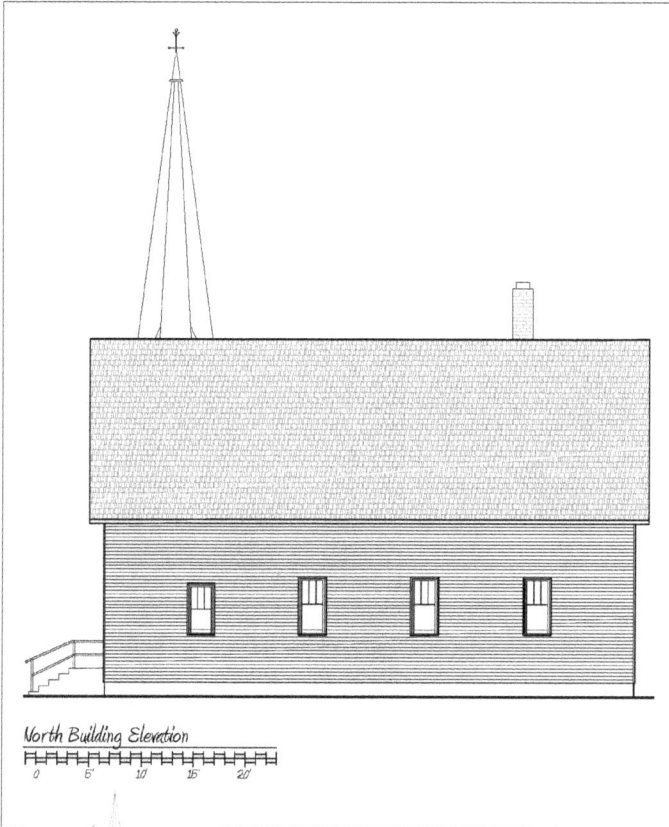

Grand Forks Lutheran Church
224 Walnut Street, Grand Forks, North Dakota
Prepared September 2011 from field measurements.

HEPPER OLSON architects

West Building Elevation

0    5'    10'    15'    20'

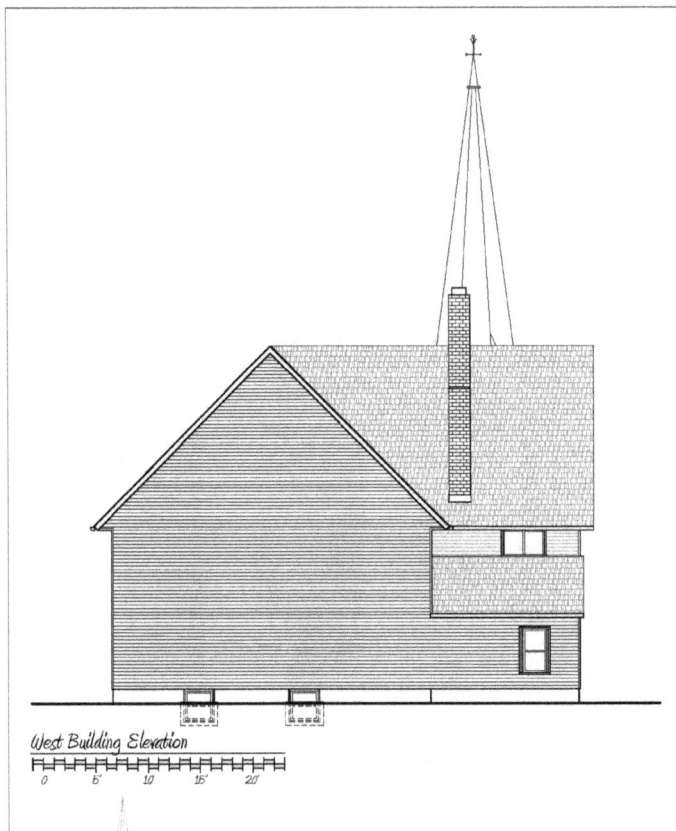

Grand Forks Lutheran Church
224 Walnut Street, Grand Forks, North Dakota
Prepared September 2011 from field measurements.

HEPPER OLSON architects

54

South Building Elevation

0  5'  10'  15'  20'

Grand Forks Lutheran Church
224 Walnut Street, Grand Forks, North Dakota
Prepared September 2011 from field measurements.

HEPPER OLSON architects

Lower Level Floor Plan

0   5'   10'   15'   20'

North

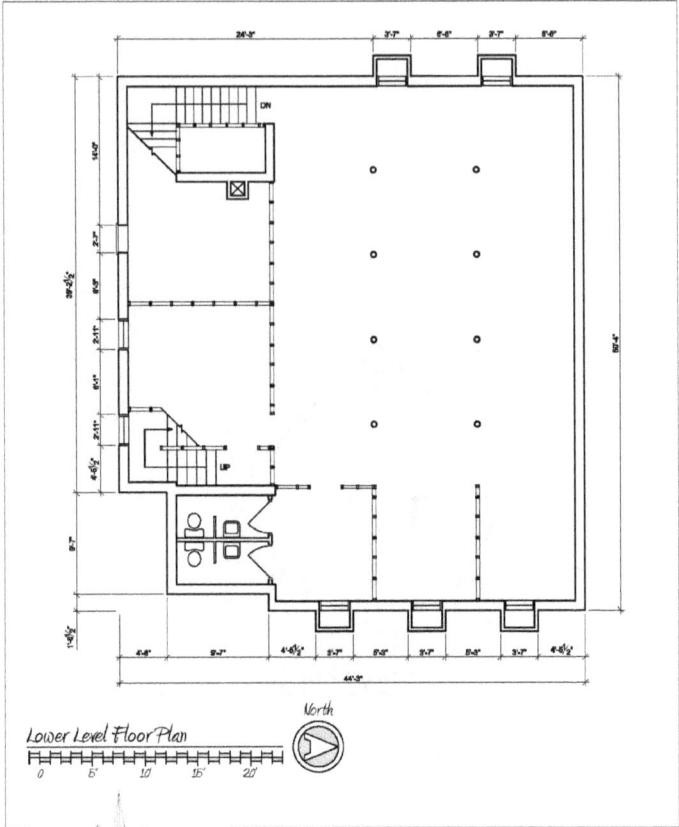

Grand Forks Lutheran Church
224 Walnut Street, Grand Forks, North Dakota
Prepared September 2011 from field measurements

HEPPER OLSON architects

56

First Level Floor Plan

0    5'    10    15'    20'

North

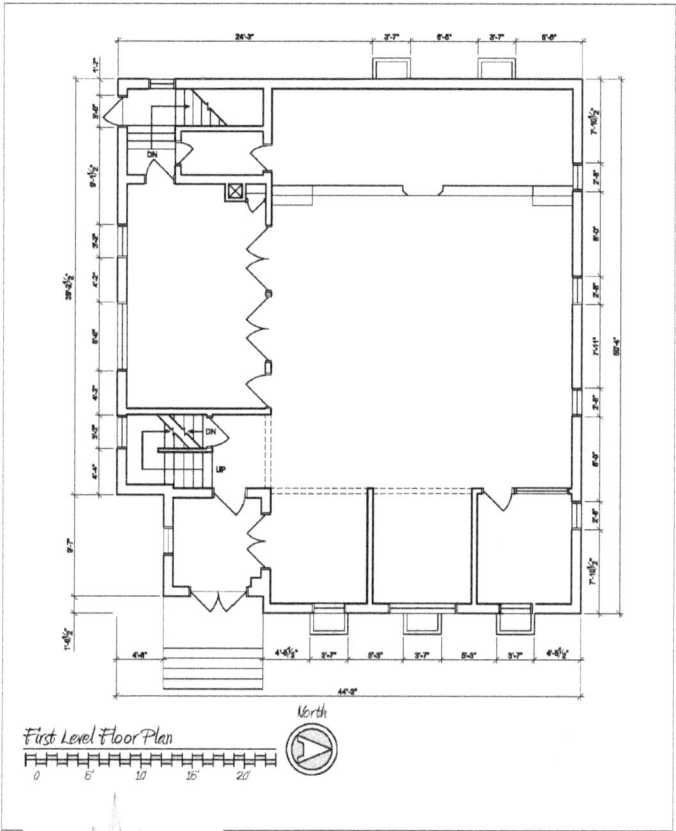

Grand Forks Lutheran Church
224 Walnut Street, Grand Forks, North Dakota
Prepared September 2011 from field measurements.

HEPPER OLSON architects

Second Level Floor Plan

0  5'  10'  15'  20'

North

Grand Forks Lutheran Church
224 Walnut Street, Grand Forks, North Dakota
Prepared September 2011 from field measurements.

HEPPER OLSON architects

58

3RD AVENUE SOUTH

ROOF SLOPE

140'-0"

92'-0"

WALNUT STREET

Site Plan / Roof Plan

North

0    10    20    30    40

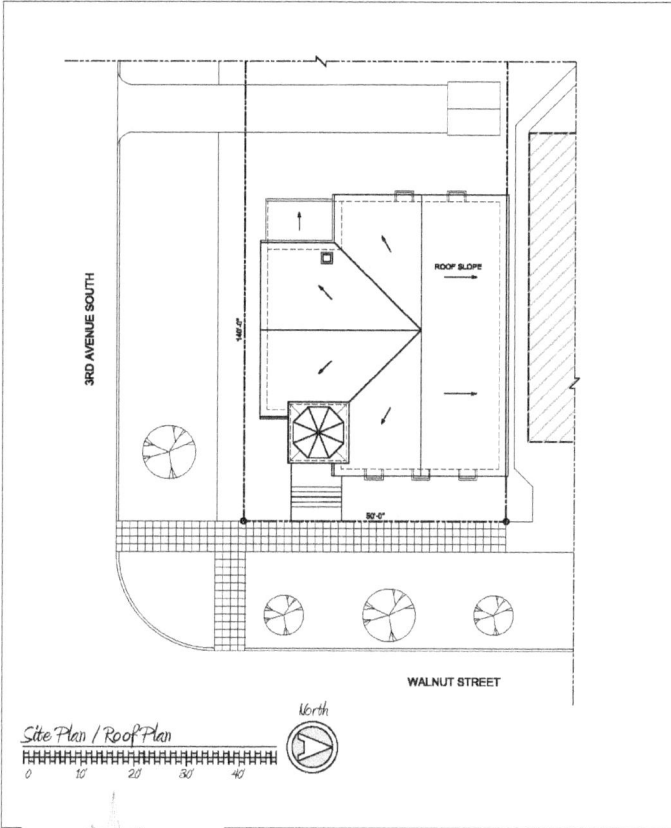

Grand Forks Lutheran Church
224 Walnut Street, Grand Forks, North Dakota
Prepared September 2011 from field measurements

HEPPER OLSON architects

The books that historians write are limited by the documents and other evidence that they have available to them. This evidence is necessarily fragmentary. Works of history depend upon primary sources that are directly tied to the subject under study, as well as secondary sources that may include secondhand information about either the topic of study or the general time and place that the topic inhabited. These secondary sources provide a broader context for past events.

Several primary sources provided the main narrative of this book. Among the more important works were histories written by members of both United Lutheran and the Grand Forks Church of God. Anna Koglin's *History of the Church of God in North Dakota* provided a broader context for larger associational activities. The online Historical Census Browser provided through the library at the University of Virginia facilitated the demographic numbers utilized in this book. Local papers such as the *Grand Forks Herald* are generally important sources for information related to community activities, and they sometimes provide editorial opinions that can give insight into some level of public opinion. The Elwyn B. Robinson Department of Special Collections at the University of North Dakota had copies of historical city maps produced by the Sanborn Map Company. These maps provided an overview of the city streetscape at various times in Grand Forks history. The personal collection of Wilferd Felchle, a member of the Grand Forks Church of God, provided many important facts in terms of both print material and early photographs. The personal reminiscence of Church of God minister S. O. Susag was enlightening in its description of the early multicultural Church of God movement in Grand Forks. Albert F. Gray's autobiography *Time and Tides on the Western Shore* included some important information about his family's part in the foundation of what would become the Grand Forks Church of God.

Three master's theses from the History Department at the University of North Dakota contributed important background information as to the early growth and religious history of Grand Forks. Alexander Aas's 1920 thesis, "The History of Grand Forks to 1889," included notable information related to early churches in Grand Forks. Anton Hillesland's 1923 thesis on "The Norwegian Lutheran Church in the Red River Valley" gave details regarding the foundation of many Lutheran churches in eastern North Dakota. Included in his study were several interviews with the first generation of Norwegian Lutherans who worshipped in these early churches. Finally, Anna Peterson's 2009 thesis provides insight into the immigrant community and its civic involvement in the rural Northern Plains. In addition to these theses, Jerome Tweton produced a pictorial history of Grand Forks in 2005 that those with an interest in the town may find of use. The leading general text of early North Dakota history continues to be Elwyn Robinson's *History of North Dakota*, originally published in 1966.

Those interested in early immigrant experiences will find Linda Mack Schloff's *And Prairie Dogs Weren't Kosher* (Minnesota Historical Society, 1996), Aagot, Raaen's *Grass of the Earth: Immigrant Life in the Dakota Territory* (Minnesota Historical Society, 1994), and Sophie Trupin's *Dakota Diaspora* (Bison Books, 1988) beneficial reads. The latter two are autobiographical in nature, while Schloff's book is a more traditional history. James Coomber and Sheldon Green's *Magnificent Churches on the Prairie* (North Dakota Institute of Regional Studies, 1996) contains not only information on immigrants, but also the religious practices and preferences of Dakota Catholics. One of the most important theoretical works that forms a foundation for the study of immigration continues to be Oscar Handlin's 1951 work titled *The Uprooted*. Finally, a couple of books that those with an interest in American Christianity may find useful are Mark Noll's general study on *A History of Christianity in the United States and Canada* (Eerdmans, 1992) and Nathan O. Hatch's *The Democratization of American Christianity* (York, 1989), which deals with the breakdown of religious hierarchies during the Second Great Awakening of the early nineteenth century.

[1] For an overview of Progressive anti-Catholic attitudes and propaganda, see Justin Nordstrom, *Danger on the Doorstep: Anti-Catholicism and American Print Culture in the Progressive Era* (Notre Dame, IN: University of Notre Dame Press, 2006). Some Southern Baptists feared a Kennedy presidency, as noted in Ricky Floyd Dobbs, "Continuities in American Anti-Catholicism: The Texas *Baptist Standard* and the Coming of the 1960 Election," *Baptist History & Heritage* 42, no. 1 (Winter 2007): 85-93.

[2] "Here's Donald Trump's Presidential Announcement Speech,"

[3] John Clark Ridpath and Selden Connor, *Life and Work of James G. Blaine* (New York: Western W. Wilson, 1893), 297.

[4] Billy Sunday, *Americanism, Address by Billy Sunday* (Philadelphia: Law Enforcement League of Philadelphia, 1922).

[5] Frederick A. Barkey, "Here Come the Boomer 'Talys': Italian Immigrants and Industrial Conflict in the Upper Kanawha Valley, 1903-1917" in *Transnational West Virginia: Ethnic Communities and Economic Change, 1840-1940*, ed. Ken Fones-Wolf and Ronald L. Lewis (Morgantown, WV: West Virginia University Press, 2002), 161-189.

[6] "History," Converge.org, https://converge.org/about/history (Accessed 18 October 2017).

[7] *Grand Forks Herald*, March 10, 1944.

[8] The church first appeared on city fire insurance maps in August 1906. The records available at United Lutheran Church do not indicate when the church was built. There were earlier churches, but they have either moved or united with other bodies.

[9] The terms "low church" and "high church" refer to the importance of such things as aesthetic beauty and liturgical rituals to a given church. High church congregations tend to favor ornate buildings with impressive artwork and elaborate rituals, while low church congregations do not.

[10] "Historical Census Browser," University of Virginia Library, http://mapserver.lib.virginia.edu/ (accessed January 24, 2012).

[11] Oscar Handlin, *The Uprooted: The Epic Story of the Great Migrations that Made the American People* (Philadelphia: University of Pennsylvania Press, 2002), 3-6, 105-128. Little, Brown, and Company originally published Handlin's work in 1951.

[12] Charles Hirschman, "The Role of Religion in the Origins and Adaptation of Immigrant Groups in the United States," in Alejandro Portes

and Josh DeWind, eds. *Rethinking Migration: New Theoretical and Empirical Perspectives* (New York: Berghahn Books, 2008) , 391-418.

[13] *The two sides of Americanism*. 1918. Theodore Roosevelt Collection. MS Am 1541 (304). Houghton Library, Harvard University. http://www.theodorerooseveltcenter.org/Research/Digital-Library/Record.aspx?libID=o280345. Theodore Roosevelt Digital Library. Dickinson State University, (accessed November 26, 2011).

[14] Nancy C. Carnevale, *A New Language, a New World: Italian Immigrants in the United States, 1890-1945* (Champaign, IL: University of Illinois Press, 2009), 46-47; Anton Hillesland, "The Norwegian Lutheran Church in the Red River Valley," (M.A. Thesis, University of North Dakota, 1923), 44. See Anna M. Peterson, "A Dash of Suffrage Spice: Rural Ethnicity Construction in the Transnational Women's Suffrage Movement," (M.A. Thesis, University of North Dakota, 2009) for further discussion of Norwegian immigrant life.

[15] "The Homestead Act (1862)," http://www.ourdocuments.gov/doc.php?doc=31 (accessed October 7, 2011).

[16] Elwyn B. Robinson, *History of North Dakota* (Lincoln, NE: University of Nebraska Press, 1966), 133-135.

[17] Bernhardt Saini-Eidukat, "North Dakota Historical Population," North Dakota State University Department of Geosciences, http://www.ndsu.edu/pubweb/~sainieid/north-dakota-historical-population.html (accessed October 5, 2011); James P. Collins, "Native Americans in the Census, 1860-1890," *Prologue* 38, No. 2 (Summer 2006), http://www.archives.gov/publications/prologue/2006/summer/indian-census.html (accessed October 5, 2011).

[18] "Historical Census Browser," University of Virginia Library, http://mapserver.lib.virginia.edu/ (accessed October 7, 2011).

[19] U.S. Census Bureau, "State and County QuickFacts," http://quickfacts.census.gov/qfd/states/38000.html, (accessed January 24, 2012). The numbers cited reflect Census Bureau estimates from 2005-2009.

[20] Sophie Trupin, *Dakota Diaspora* (Lincoln and London: Bison Books, 1988), 5-9, 15-17; Linda Mack Schloff, *"And Prairie Dogs Weren't Kosher": Jewish Women in the Upper Midwest since 1855* (St. Paul: Minnesota Historical Society Press, 1996), 7.

[21] Diana Everett, "Germans from Russia," *Encyclopedia of Oklahoma History & Culture* (Oklahoma Historical Society, 2007),

http://digital.library.okstate.edu/encyclopedia/entries/G/GE008.html (accessed October 28, 2011).

22 Robinson, 146.

23 E. Clifford Nelson and Eugene L. Fevold, *The Lutheran Church among Norwegian-Americans: A History of the Evangelical Lutheran Church, Volume I, 1825-1890* (Minneapolis: Augsburg Publishing House, 1960), 1-12, 47-48.

24 The term Haugean from this point forward refers to those who followed the teachings of Hans Nielsen Hauge in America.

25 James Coomber and Sheldon Green, *Magnificent Churches on the Prairie: A Story of Immigrant Priests, Builders, and Homesteaders* (Fargo: North Dakota Institute for Regional Studies, 1996), 13-15, 25, 37-39, 75.

26 Alexander Aas, "The History of the City of Grand Forks to 1889," (M.A. Thesis, University of North Dakota, 1920), 44.

27 Delores Hayden, *The Power of Place: Urban Landscapes as Public History* (Cambridge, MA, and London: MIT Press, 1997), 34.

28 Robinson, 130.

29 Aas, 36-42.

30 "Grand Forks, Dakota," Sanborn Map & Publishing Co., 1884. North Dakota Sanborn Fire Insurance Map Collection (hereafter ND Sanborn Maps), Folder 519. Orin G. Libby Manuscript Collection, Chester Fritz Library, University of North Dakota, Grand Forks, ND.

31 ND Sanborn Maps, 1888, 1892, Folder 519.

32 Minutes of Business Meeting, First Baptist Church, Grand Forks, Dakota Territory, December 3, 1885. First Baptist Church, Grand Forks collection (hereafter designated as First Baptist Papers), Folder 1. Orin G. Libby Manuscript Collection, Chester Fritz Library, University of North Dakota, Grand Forks, ND; Minutes of Business Meeting, June 30, 1908. First Baptist Papers, Folder 2.

33 ND Sanborn Maps, 1888.

34 Lansing, Michael, *The Faith of Our Forebears: 100 Years at Mount Olive Lutheran Church* (Minneapolis: Mount Olive Lutheran Church, 2009), 1-2.

35 *A Century, "Blessed to Be a Blessing": A Heritage Dedicated to the Future Congregation* (United Lutheran Church, 1979), 1. Elywn B. Robinson Department of Special Collections, University of North Dakota, Grand Forks, ND.

36 Barbara Handy-Marchello, "Introduction to the Reprint Edition," in Aagot Raaen, *Grass of the Earth: Immigrant Life in the Dakota Country* (St. Paul, MN: Minnesota Historical Society Press, 1994), xxi.

[37] "Grand Forks History," The City of Grand Forks, North Dakota, http://www.grandforksgov.com/gfgov/home.nsf/Pages/History, (accessed January 24, 2012).

[38] *Blessed to Be a Blessing*, 1-3.

[39] Ibid.; Anton Hillesland, "The Norwegian Lutheran Church in the Red River Valley," (M.A. Thesis, University of North Dakota, 1923), 44; Nelson and Fevold, 296-297

[40] *Blessed to Be a Blessing"*, 1-3.

[41] Hillesland, 116.

[42] Ibid, 2.

[43] ND Sanborn Maps, 1892, 1897, 1901, 1906.

[44] Robert C. Wiederaenders, *Historical Guide to Lutheran Church Bodies of North America*. 2nd ed. (St. Louis: Lutheran Historical Conference, 1998), 34-37.

[45] Nelson and Fevold, Volume 1, 13-23.

[46] Ibid., 126.

[47] Ibid., 190.

[48] *Blessed to Be a Blessing"*, 2.

[49] Wiederaenders, 36. The three smaller synods that made up the new United Synod were the Anti-Missourian Brotherhood, the Conference for the Norwegian-Danish Evangelical Lutheran Church in America, and the Norwegian-Danish Augustana Synod in America (later simply the Norwegian-Augustana Synod).

[50] Ibid., 140.

[51] Hillesland, 111.

[52] *Blessed to Be a Blessing"*, 2; O. M. Norlie, *Norsk Lutherske Menigheter i Amerika, 1843-1916, Volume 2* (Minneapolis: Augsburg Publishing House, 1918), 61. The cost in 2016 dollars is taken from a calculator located at http://www.measuringworth.com/uscompare/relativevalue.php. This website is maintained by two economists from the University of Illinois at Chicago, Lawrence H. Officer and Samuel H. Williamson. The number used above is related to the basic value of money in relation to inflation. The site also includes varied values based upon wealth, projects, and commodities. This particular calculator only tracks inflation to 2016.

[53] *Blessed to Be a Blessing"*, 5-6, 22.

[54] Minutes of Business Meeting, December 9, 1903. First Baptist Papers, Folder 2.

[55] ND Sanborn Maps, 1906.

[56] *Blessed to Be a Blessing"*, 3.

[57] Ibid., 7.

[58] Ibid.

[59] Ibid., 42.

[60] E. Clifford Nelson, *The Lutheran Church among Norwegian-Americans: A History of the Evangelical Lutheran Church, Volume II, 1890-1959* (Minneapolis: Augsburg Publishing House, 1960), 3-4, 22.

[61] Ibid., 183, 212-213

[62] *"Blessed to Be a Blessing"*, 8-9.

[63] Hillesland, 25.

[64] Ibid., 5, 8-9.

[65] Stephen J. Lee, "United—for 125 Years," *Grand Forks Herald,* October 23, 2004.

[66] Mark Noll, *A History of Christianity in the United States and Canada* (Grand Rapids, MI: Eerdmans, 1992), 165-190.

[67] Nathan O. Hatch, *The Democratization of American Christianity* (New Haven: Yale University Press, 1989), 3-16, 220-226.

[68] There are multiple denominational and nondenominational movements that have taken the name of the Church of God. The Grand Forks Church of God is affiliated with the Church of God headquartered in Anderson, Indiana. A more Pentecostal denomination with the Church of God name has its headquarters in Cleveland, Tennessee.

[69] William Kostlevy, *Historical Dictionary of the Holiness Movement* (Lanham, MD: Scarecrow Press, 2009), xxxvii-xxxviii, 55-58.

[70] "Our History," http://www.chog.org/our-history (accessed November 6, 2011)

[71] Albert F. Gray, *Time and Tides on the Western Shore: An Autobiography of Albert F. Gray* (Springfield, OH: Reformation Publishers, 1966), 12-13. According to Wilferd Felchle in *History of the First Church of God, Grand Forks, North Datoka*, the address of this house was initially 612 9th Avenue. The original house no longer stands at the lot, according to a building permit dated 1904.

[72] Wilferd Felchle, et al, *History of the First Church of God, Grand Forks, North Dakota: Christ Our Heritage—Christ Our Future* (Grand Forks, ND, 1995), 5. The August 1906 Sanborn map for Grand Forks indicated this "Church of God Chapel" at 125 Cottonwood. The January 1901 map indicated that this building belonged to a "Norwegian Sunday School," which follows the pattern of the utilization of small wood-framed churches by immigrant congregations.

[73] Earl E. Cairns, *Christianity through the Centuries: A History of the Christian Church, 3rd Ed.* (Grand Rapids, MI: Zondervan, 1996), 428-429.

[74] Anna Emilie Koglin, *History of the Church of God in North Dakota* (n.d.), 25-26.

[75] Ibid., 25.

[76] Felchle, 5-6, 12.

[77] S. O. Susag, *Personal Experiences of S. O. Susag* (Minneapolis, 1966), 5, 16,47. Elwyn B. Robinson Deparment of Special Collections, Chester Fritz Library, University of North Dakota, Grand Forks, ND.

[78] Arlo F. Newell, *A Servant in God's Kingdom: The Story of Max R. Gaulke's Life Poured out in Kingdom Work* (Anderson, IN: Warner Press, 1995), 20.

[79] Newell, 51-60, 74-75, 96-113, 206-211, 225, 263.

[80] Gray, 10-16.

[81] Undated newspaper clipping from personal scrapbook of Wilferd Felchle.

[82] Gray, 98-99, 171-176.

[83] "Flames Sweep Church," News clipping from personal scrapbook of Wilferd Felchle.

[84] The National Oceanic and Atmospheric Administration (NOAA) indicates that the climate division of which Grand forks is a part generally saw enough precipitation in the mid-1940s. This data disputes Koglin's assertion. See NOAA Satellite and Information Service, http://www.ncdc.noaa.gov/temp-and-precip/time-series/index.php (accessed March 8, 2012).

[85] Anna Emilie Koglin, *History of the Grand Forks Church of God, Grand Forks, North Dakota, 1895-1970* (Grand Forks, ND: Grand Forks Church of God, 1970), 3-4. North Dakota Church History Collection. Box 2, Folder 16. Orin G. Libby Manuscript Collection. Elwyn B. Robinson Department of Special Collections. Grand Forks, ND.

[86] Ibid., 4.

[87] "In Memory of Our Dear Brother Ray L. Finley," *Forerunner* (October 1953), 1, 12.

[88] Felchle, 9-10.

[89] *You Are Invited to the First Church of God* (Grand Forks, ND, n.d).
Most Christian denominations follow a particular creed or confession, such as the Nicene Creed or the Augsburg or Westminster Confessions of Faith. These creeds and confessions enumerate the particular doctrines of the denomination or body and generally include biblical references to support their

beliefs. Some groups, including the Church of God, Anderson, refuse to accept such creeds, however.

[90] Marilyn Hagerty, "See the Light: GF Church Lights up Season with Huge Christmas Tree," *Grand Forks Herald*, December 6, 1993. Felchle typed up a personal remembrance of the singing Christmas tree and included it in his personal scrapbook of the Grand Forks Church of God's history.

[91] Thomas Martzall, interview by author, Grand Forks, ND, September 30, 2011.

[92] "What Are CLTs?" *Grand Forks Community Land Trust*, http://www.gfclt.org/what-are-clts.html, (accessed March 18, 2012).

[93] Ibid.

Figures

Figure 1: Church on Fire. *Grand Forks Herald*, March 10, 1944.
(Courtesy of *Grand Forks Herald*)

Figure 2: Grand Forks Steam Laundry
(courtesy of Wilferd Felchle)

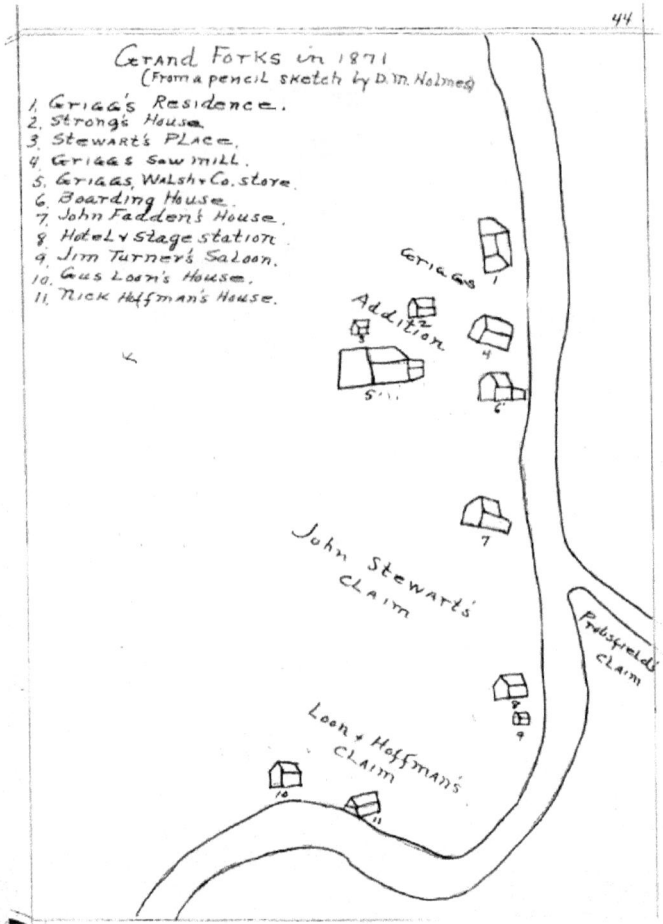

Figure 3: Alexander Aas, "The History of the City of Grand Forks to 1889," (M.A. Thesis, University of North Dakota, 1920), 44.

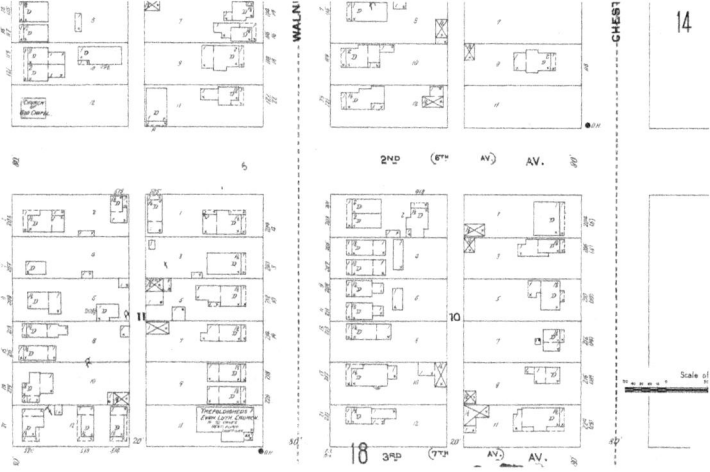

Figure 4: Sanborn Map & Publishing Co., Grand Forks, North Dakota, 1906. Folio 13 (Courtesy of UND Special Collections)

Figure 5: Mr. and Mrs. Peterman (courtesy of Wilferd Felchle)

Figure 6: Church of God on Cottonwood (Courtesy of Wilferd Felchle)

Figure 7: Nelson Family (Courtesy of Wilferd Felchle)

Figure 8: Nelson Family in the snow (Courtesy of Wilferd Felchle)

Figure 9: Gaulke Family, Max in stripes (Courtesy of Wilferd Felchle)

Figures 10: Lulu Pinkerton (courtesy of Wilferd Felchle)

Figure 11:  Mr. and Mrs. Bahr (courtesy of Wilferd Felchle)

Figure 12: Remodeled Church after fire (courtesy of Wilferd Felchle)

Figure 13—Church basement with baptistery (author's image)

## ABOUT THE AUTHOR

Chris Price teaches history at Colby Community College, where he has served on the faculty since 2013. He holds an MA in history from Marshall University in Huntington, West Virginia, and a Doctor of Arts in history from the University of North Dakota in Grand Forks. He currently lives in Northwest Kansas with his wife and two daughters.

www.ingramcontent.com/pod-product-compliance
Lightning Source LLC
Chambersburg PA
CBHW060339050426
42449CB00011B/2791